What's the Best Sports Trivia Book?

1,500 Questions in 6 Categories

David Fickes

D1056641

Printed in the United States of America

First Printing: 2018

Introduction

By nature, I tend to collect trivia without trying. Until relatively recently, I had never sought out trivia; however, after creating a holiday trivia presentation for a community party and then showing it at one of our fitness studio's spinning classes, I found myself creating weekly trivia. The cycling clients enjoyed the diversion of answering questions while they exercised, so I continued.

What you find in most trivia is a lot of erroneous or outdated information or questions that are so simple or esoteric that they aren't interesting. It is difficult to come up with interesting questions that are at the right level of difficulty that a wide variety of people can enjoy them, and they are something that you feel you should know or want to know. I have tried to ensure that the information is as accurate as possible, and to retain its accuracy, I have also tried to avoid questions whose answers can easily change with time. Additional details are also frequently included to expand on the basic answer and add even more to your knowledge

There are 1,500 questions in 6 categories: Miscellaneous, Baseball, Basketball, Football, Hockey, and Olympics. To make it quick and easy to test yourself or others without initially seeing the answers, each category is divided into short quizzes with 10 questions followed by their answers.

This is book 3 of my *What's the Best Trivia?* series; I hope you enjoy it, and if you do, look for other books in the series covering a variety of trivia topics.

Contents

Miscellaneous

Quiz 1

1) Who won the 2014 men's field hockey World Cup?

2) How many furlongs are there in a mile?

3) In any NCAA division, what is the record for most consecutive team national championships in any men's or women's sport?

4) How many points is a ringer worth in horseshoes?

5) Who won the 2011 women's soccer World Cup?

6) Who is the only men's wildcard entrant to win Wimbledon?

7) At what school did Tiger Woods play NCAA golf?

8) What outdoor game is won by "pegging out"?

9) In what country did volleyball originate?

10) Who held seven American running records from 2,000 to 10,000 meters when he died in a 1975 car crash?

Quiz 1 Answers

1) Australia

2) Eight

3) 31 years – Kenyon College in Division III men's swimming and diving from 1980–2010

4) Three

5) Japan

6) Goran Ivanisevic – 2001

7) Stanford – He was the 1996 NCAA individual golf champion and then left to turn professional.

8) Croquet

9) United States

10) Steve Prefontaine

Quiz 2

1) What is the New Zealand rugby team called?

2) The son of what famous entertainer won the 1981 U.S. Amateur Golf

Championship?

3) How many players are there on a cricket side?

4) In 1965, who was the first foreign born golfer in 38 years to win the U.S. Open?

5) Who is Edson Arantes do Nascimento better known as?

6) What was the first country to win two consecutive women's soccer World Cups?

7) What bowler has the most career PBA wins?

8) Who is the only person to win the calendar year tennis Grand Slam twice?

9) Who is the first driver to ever complete the Triple Crown of Motorsport consisting of winning the Indianapolis 500, 24 Hours of Le Mans, and the Monaco Grand Prix over a career?

10) Who was the first golfer to wear the green jacket as the winner of the Masters?

Quiz 2 Answers

1) All Blacks

2) Bing Crosby - His son Nathaniel won at San Francisco's Olympic Club just miles from his home.

3) 11

4) Gary Player

5) Pele – Brazilian soccer player

6) Germany – 2003 and 2007

7) Walter Ray Williams Jr. – 47 wins

8) Rod Laver – 1962 and 1969

9) Graham Hill (Great Britain) – 1963 Monaco Grand Prix, 1966 Indianapolis 500, 1972 Le Mans

10) Sam Snead - The jacket was introduced in 1949.

Quiz 3

1) Mintonette was the original name of what sport?

2) Who is the only male or female six-time winner of the Associated Press Athlete of the year?

3) Who was the first left-handed male golfer to win a Major

Championship?

4) What athlete has appeared on the Wheaties box the most times?

5) What was the first team to win two consecutive women's field hockey World Cups?

6) Who was the first African American to win the Wimbledon men's singles title?

7) What country won the first men's soccer World Cup?

8) What title has been won by the rider who wears the polka dot jersey in the Tour de France?

9) What was the first U.S. college sport to name an All-American team?

10) Who was the first *Sports Illustrated* Sportsperson of the Year?

Quiz 3 Answers

1) Volleyball

2) Babe Didrikson - 1932, 1945, 1946, 1947, 1950, 1954

3) Sir Bob Charles (New Zealand) - 1963 British Open

4) Michael Jordan – 18 times

5) Netherlands - 1983 and 1986

6) Arthur Ashe - 1975

7) Uruguay

8) King of the Mountains

9) Football – 1889

10) Roger Bannister – first sub-four-minute mile

Quiz 4

1) What is the world's oldest tennis tournament?

2) What year was the first cross-country skiing World Cup competition?

3) What year was the Davis Cup tennis competition first held?

4) What is the length of a tennis court in feet?

5) What was the first team to win three consecutive cricket World Cups?

6) What sport originated the term southpaw?

7) For racing purposes, what is the birthday of all horses in the Northern Hemisphere?

8) Who was the first athlete to appear anywhere on a Wheaties box?

9) What year was the first Oxford and Cambridge rowing race held?

10) What actor finished runner-up in the Le Mans 24-hour auto race?

Quiz 4 Answers

1) Wimbledon - 1877

2) 1981

3) 1900

4) 78 feet

5) Australia - 1999, 2003, 2007

6) Boxing - Left-handed fighters were said to use a southpaw stance; no one is quite sure why but hitting someone with a left came to be known as a southpaw punch.

7) January 1 - A horse born on December 31 is one year old on January 1.

8) Lou Gehrig - He was on the back in 1934.

9) 1829

10) Paul Newman - 1979

Quiz 5

1) Who was the first driver in NASCAR history to win 20 races in a season?

2) In a game of horseshoes, how many feet apart are the stakes?

3) What is the oldest of horse racing's Triple Crown races?

4) Who was the first PGA golfer to shoot their age in a tournament round?

5) Who was the first woman to win the Sullivan Award which is given annually to the most outstanding U.S. amateur athlete?

6) What golfer holds the record for most PGA tour wins in a season?

7) Horse racing's Triple Crown has only been won once in consecutive years; what years?

8) In 1935, what athlete set world records in three different events in 45 minutes?

9) What male or female singles figure skater has won the most U.S. Championships?

10) Who was the last man to win a calendar year tennis Grand Slam?

Quiz 5 Answers

1) Richard Petty – 27 in 1967

2) 40 feet

3) Belmont Stakes – 1867

4) Sam Snead – He shot a 67 at the 1979 Quad Cities Open.

5) Ann Curtis – 1944 for swimming

6) Byron Nelson – 18 wins in 1945

7) 1977 and 1978 – Seattle Slew and Affirmed

8) Jesse Owens – At a Big Ten track and field meet, he set world records in the long jump, 220-yard sprint, and 220-yard low hurdles and tied the world record for the 100-yard dash.

9) Dick Button – seven consecutive titles from 1946-1952

10) Rod Laver – 1969

Quiz 6

1) Who is the only world heavyweight boxing champion to finish his career undefeated?

2) How many horses have won racing's Triple Crown?

3) What NASCAR driver had the most victories from 1960-1969?

4) Who was the first hockey player to win the *Sports Illustrated* Sportsperson of the Year?

5) Who won the 2015 men's rugby World Cup?

6) Who was the first gymnast to win the *Sports Illustrated* Sportsperson of the Year?

7) Who is the first world boxing champion to hold a PhD degree?

8) Who was the first male alpine skier to win seven consecutive overall World Cup titles?

9) Who was the last male to win four Grand Slam singles tennis tournaments in a row?

10) Who is the only person to be number one in the world in both table tennis and tennis?

Quiz 6 Answers

1) Rocky Marciano – He retired in 1956 with a 49-0 record.

2) 13 - Sir Barton (1919), Gallant Fox (1930), Omaha (1935), War Admiral (1937), Whirlaway (1941), Count Fleet (1943), Assault (1946), Citation (1948), Secretariat (1973), Seattle Slew (1977), Affirmed (1978), American Pharoah (2015), Justify (2018)

3) Richard Petty - 101

4) Bobby Orr - 1970

5) New Zealand

6) Mary Lou Retton - 1984

7) Vitali Klitschko - He was a three-time world heavyweight champion starting in 1999 and ending in 2013 and got his PhD in sports science in 2000. He has also served as mayor of Kiev and as a member of the Ukrainian parliament.

8) Marcel Hirscher (Austria) – 2012 to 2018

9) Novak Djokovic - 2015 Wimbledon to 2016 French Open

10) Fred Perry – He won the 1929 world championship in table tennis and was the first player in tennis to win a career grand slam including three straight Wimbledon titles from 1934-1936.

Quiz 7

1) What are the only two days during the year where there are no MLB, NFL, NHL or NBA games played?

2) What is the diameter of a golf hole?

3) Who was the first European to win the Masters golf tournament?

4) What year was the first sanctioned NASCAR championship season?

5) What NASCAR driver had the most victories from 2000-2009?

6) Who was the first unseeded man to win Wimbledon?

7) In outdoor field lacrosse, how many players are on a team?

8) Who was the first male athlete to win 10 career gold medals in the IAAF World Track and Field Championships?

9) What is the name of the trophy given to the winner of the men's British Open golf tournament?

10) Where did curling originate?

Quiz 7 Answers

1) The Monday before and the Wednesday after the MLB All-Star game - The MLB All-Star game is always played on a Tuesday, and there are no MLB games the day before or after, and MLB is the only professional sport played in July.
2) 4 ¼ inches
3) Severiano Ballesteros (Spain) - 1980
4) 1949
5) Jimmie Johnson – 48 wins
6) Boris Becker - 1985
7) 10 - three attackers, three midfielders, three defenders, goalie
8) Usain Bolt - Jamaica
9) The Claret Jug - first presented in 1872
10) Scotland

Quiz 8

1) Who is the only American who has won an overall cross-country skiing World Cup championship?
2) What year was the first women's soccer World Cup?
3) What country won the first women's rugby World Cup?
4) Who was the first professional boxer to win world titles in three weight divisions?
5) Who won the 2017 women's rugby World Cup?
6) The open era in tennis began when professionals could compete in tournaments along with amateurs; what year did it start?
7) In 1932, what athlete single-handedly won the AAU national track and field team championship?
8) Who was the last woman to win a calendar year tennis Grand Slam?
9) What were table tennis balls originally made from?
10) Women's world golf rankings were introduced in 2006; who was the first official number one woman in the world?

Quiz 8 Answers

1) Bill Koch - 1982

2) 1991

3) United States – 1991

4) Bob Fitzsimmons – middleweight (1891), heavyweight (1897), light heavyweight (1903)

5) New Zealand

6) 1968

7) Babe Didrikson – She competed in eight out of ten events; she won five and tied for first in a sixth event; she won the team championship despite being the only member of her team.

8) Steffi Graf – 1988

9) Cork – from wine bottles

10) Annika Sorenstam – Sweden

Quiz 9

1) Of all the players in North American men's professional sports, who has won the most MVP awards?

2) In the post 1968 open era, who are the only two tennis players who have won six consecutive Grand Slam singles tournaments?

3) What driver holds the record for most consecutive Formula One race wins?

4) What male golfer has finished runner-up the most times in the four major championships?

5) Who was the first driver to win two consecutive Indianapolis 500 races?

6) In darts, what is the highest score possible with three darts?

7) What is the only sport where you can see teams defending goals of different sizes?

8) What is the fastest racquet sport?

9) In what country was the famous Rumble in the Jungle boxing match between Muhammad Ali and George Foreman fought?

10) What NCAA Division I school has the record for most consecutive team national championships in any men's or women's sport?

Quiz 9 Answers

1) Wayne Gretzky – nine

2) Margaret Court (1969 U.S. Open to 1971 Australian Open) and

Martina Navratilova (1983 Wimbledon to 1984 U.S. Open)

3) Sebastian Vettel (Germany) - nine consecutive wins in 2013

4) Jack Nicklaus - 19 times

5) Wilbur Shaw - 1939, 1940

6) 180 – three triple 20s

7) Water polo – The goal at the deep end is smaller than the goal at the shallow end.

8) Badminton – The shuttlecock can travel over 200 mph.

9) Zaire

10) Arkansas - 12 straight men's indoor track and field championships from 1984-1995

Quiz 10

1) Who won the 2018 women's field hockey World Cup?

2) Who won the 2011 men's rugby World Cup?

3) Who was the 20-year-old amateur American golfer who won the U.S. Open in 1913 and started a boom in golf in the U.S.?

4) What is the straightaway opposite the finish line in horse racing called?

5) The Borg-Warner trophy is awarded for winning what?

6) In what sport is the Iroquois Cup awarded?

7) What year was the first America's Cup sailing competition?

8) What year did Jack Nicklaus win his last major championship?

9) What NASCAR driver had the most victories from 1950-1959?

10) Who is the only male to win six consecutive Grand Slam singles tennis tournaments?

Quiz 10 Answers

1) Netherlands

2) New Zealand

3) Francis Ouimet

4) Backstretch

5) Indianapolis 500

6) Lacrosse

7) 1851 – It was originally called the 100 Guinea Cup but was renamed to America's Cup after the boat *America* won the first competition.

8) 1986 – Masters

9) Herb Thomas – 48 wins

10) Don Budge – 1937 Wimbledon to 1938 U.S. Championships

Quiz 11

1) What boxer won world titles in the largest number of weight divisions?

2) What was the first team to win two consecutive men's field hockey World Cups?

3) What is the longest length of time any sports trophy has been successfully defended?

4) What sports hero wore a cabbage leaf under his cap?

5) Who is the youngest world heavyweight boxing champion ever?

6) Who has appeared on the most *Sports Illustrated* covers?

7) Who won the 2010 men's field hockey World Cup?

8) What sport is played on the largest field?

9) What are the five events in an alpine skiing World Cup competition?

10) Who was the first athlete to appear on the front of the Wheaties box?

Quiz 11 Answers

1) Manny Pacquiao – Eight divisions – flyweight, super bantamweight, featherweight, super featherweight, lightweight, light welterweight, welterweight, super welterweight

2) Pakistan – 1978 and 1982

3) 132 years – The America's Cup for sailing was held by the United States from its start in 1851 until Australia won in 1983.

4) Babe Ruth – He put chilled cabbage leaves under his cap to keep cool.

5) Mike Tyson – 20 years old

6) Michael Jordan – 50 covers

7) Australia

8) Polo – 300 yards by 160 yards

9) Slalom, giant slalom, super G, downhill, and combined (downhill and slalom)

10) Bob Richards in 1958 – He was the 1952 and 1956 Olympic pole vault gold medalist.

Quiz 12

1) Bowler Walter Ray Williams Jr. has won many PBA titles and is also a nine-time world champion in what other sport?

2) Who won the first women's soccer World Cup?

3) Who has won the most consecutive Wimbledon singles titles?

4) What is the only sports team to play on all seven continents?

5) What was the first country to win two consecutive men's rugby World Cups?

6) The Greek god Apollo accidentally killed his friend Hyacinthus while practicing what sporting event?

7) What bowler has won the PBA Player of the Year the most times?

8) What is the only U.S. city to win three of the four major professional sports championships in the same year?

9) Who won the 2014 men's soccer World Cup?

10) Who won the 2014 women's field hockey World Cup?

Quiz 12 Answers

1) Horseshoes

2) United States

3) Martina Navratilova – six consecutive titles from 1982–1987

4) Harlem Globetrotters

5) New Zealand – 2011 and 2015

6) Discus

7) Walter Ray Williams Jr. – seven times

8) Detroit – In 1935, it won the NFL, NBA, and NHL titles.

9) Germany

10) Netherlands

Quiz 13

1) How many horses are there on a polo team?
2) What jockey rode Secretariat to his 1973 Triple Crown win?
3) What was the first team to win two consecutive cricket World Cups?
4) What famous American statesman earned an honorary induction into the International Swimming Hall of Fame?
5) Who won the 2007 women's soccer World Cup?
6) Who is the only tennis player to have won the U.S. Open singles title on three different surfaces (grass, clay, hardcourt)?
7) What is the only country that has played in every men's soccer World Cup tournament?
8) What year was the famous "Battle of the Sexes" tennis match between Billie Jean King and Bobby Riggs?
9) Who was the first auto racer to win the *Sports Illustrated* Sportsperson of the Year?
10) What NASCAR driver had the most victories from 1990–1999?

Quiz 13 Answers

1) Four
2) Ron Turcotte
3) West Indies – 1975 and 1979
4) Benjamin Franklin – He had a lifelong love of swimming and was an ardent proponent of it and invented some swim fins.
5) Germany
6) Jimmy Connors
7) Brazil
8) 1973
9) Jackie Stewart – 1973
10) Jeff Gordon – 49

Quiz 14

1) Who has the most career LPGA Majors wins?
2) Who is the oldest golfer to win a PGA tour event?
3) What year did Roger Bannister run the first sub-four-minute mile?

4) Who was the first thoroughbred horse to win $1 million?

5) What sport originated the term hat trick?

6) Who was the first American to win the Tour de France bicycle race?

7) Singer Johnny Mathis was a world class athlete in what event?

8) Where is the world's largest bullfighting ring?

9) Pete Sampras won 14 Grand Slam singles titles, but he never won which Grand Slam tournament?

10) Who are the only three male or female tennis players that have won singles, doubles, and mixed doubles titles at each of the Grand Slam tournaments in their career?

Quiz 14 Answers

1) Patty Berg - 15 from 1937-1958

2) Sam Snead - He was 52 years old when he won the 1965 Greater Greensboro Open.

3) 1954

4) Citation – last Triple Crown winner prior to Secretariat

5) Cricket - The term first appeared in 1858 in England when H. H. Stephenson took three wickets with three consecutive balls; fans held a collection for him and presented him with a hat bought with the proceeds.

6) Greg LeMond – 1986

7) High jump – He was invited to the Olympic trials when he got a recording contract; his major high jump competitor in the San Francisco Bay area where he grew up was future NBA Hall of Fame star Bill Russell.

8) Mexico City

9) French Open - The 1996 semi-final was the closest he got.

10) Doris Hart, Margaret Court, and Martina Navratilova

Quiz 15

1) Who was the first tennis player ever expelled from a Grand Slam tournament?

2) Who was the lightest boxer to ever hold the world heavyweight title?

3) What horse has won the Grand National Steeplechase the most

times?

4) What female alpine skier has the most World Cup downhill season titles?

5) What Wimbledon singles champion had a part in a John Wayne film?

6) Who won the 2015 cricket World Cup?

7) What year was the first Kentucky Derby run?

8) Who won the 2011 cricket World Cup?

9) Who was the first non-American golfer to win the Masters?

10) What was the first sport to be filmed?

Quiz 15 Answers

1) John McEnroe - 1990 Australian Open
2) Bob Fitzsimmons - 167 pounds when he won the title in 1897
3) Red Rum – three wins in 1973, 1974, and 1977
4) Lindsey Vonn - U.S.
5) Althea Gibson - *The Horse Soldiers* in 1959
6) Australia
7) 1875
8) India
9) Gary Player – 1961
10) Boxing – 1894

Quiz 16

1) Who is the only person to win six consecutive tennis Grand Slam singles tournaments and not complete a calendar year Grand Slam?

2) What country won the first men's rugby World Cup?

3) Who holds the record for most consecutive PGA tour wins?

4) What is the lowest score ever recorded for an 18-hole round of golf in a PGA tournament?

5) Who was the first person to win the *Sports Illustrated* Sportsperson of the Year twice?

6) Who was the first tennis player to win the *Sports Illustrated* Sportsperson of the Year?

7) What was the first country to win five men's soccer World Cups?

8) What male alpine skier has the most overall World Cup titles?

9) What are the first two countries to win consecutive men's soccer World Cups?

10) What is the name of the biennial men's golf competition between teams from Europe and the United States?

Quiz 16 Answers

1) Martina Navratilova – 1983 Wimbledon to 1984 U.S. Open

2) New Zealand – 1987

3) Byron Nelson – 11 in 1945

4) 58 – Jim Furyk in 2016

5) Tiger Woods – 1996 and 2000

6) Billie Jean King – 1972

7) Brazil – 1958, 1962, 1970, 1994, 2002

8) Marcel Hirscher (Austria)

9) Italy (1934, 1938) and Brazil (1958, 1962)

10) Ryder Cup – established in 1927

Quiz 17

1) Why was Brazil allowed to permanently keep the men's soccer World Cup trophy after their 1970 victory?

2) How high is a soccer goal?

3) Who was the first woman to swim the English Channel?

4) Who was the first filly to win the Kentucky Derby?

5) In horse racing, which of the Triple Crown races is the shortest?

6) In golf, what do you call a score of four under par on a single hole?

7) Who was the second person to run a sub-four-minute mile?

8) In what sport did the word stymie originate?

9) Although no woman has completed a four or five major calendar Grand Slam in golf, one woman won all three majors that were contested in a calendar year; who was she?

10) Who was the first woman to win the *Sports Illustrated* Sportsperson of the Year?

Quiz 17 Answers

1) It was Brazil's third win. It was stipulated at the time the tournament was founded that if any nation won the trophy three times they would be allowed to keep it permanently.

2) Eight feet

3) Gertrude Ederle – 1926

4) Regret – 1915

5) Preakness – 1 3/16 miles

6) Condor – There have only been four verified; all were hole in ones on par five holes.

7) John Landy (Australia) – 1954

8) Golf – Until 1952 when the rules changed, balls had to remain in place, so you could be stymied by having another player's ball between your ball and the hole; you had to loft your ball over the other ball.

9) Mildred "Babe" Didrikson Zaharias – 1950

10) Billie Jean King – 1972

Quiz 18

1) What was the name of the original men's soccer World Cup trophy that was awarded from 1930–1970?

2) What were golf balls originally made of?

3) Who was the first female alpine skier to win three consecutive overall World Cup titles?

4) What country has won the most cricket World Cups?

5) Who was the first driver to win two NASCAR championships?

6) Who was the first U.S. high school athlete to run a mile in under four minutes?

7) In what country did table tennis originate?

8) What year was the first alpine skiing World Cup competition?

9) The Emperors Cup is awarded in what sport?

10) Who are the only two males to win all four tennis Grand Slam singles tournaments during their career plus the Olympic singles gold medal?

Quiz 18 Answers

1) Jules Rimet Trophy – It was named after FIFA president Jules Rimet who initiated the tournament; it had to be replaced after Brazil won the trophy to keep permanently in 1970.

2) Wood – In the early 17th century, wood was replaced by a feather ball consisting of boiled feathers compressed inside a stitched leather cover.

3) Annmarie Moser–Proll (Austria) – 1971 to 1973

4) Australia

5) Herb Thomas – 1951, 1953

6) Jim Ryun – 1964

7) England – late 19th century

8) 1967

9) Sumo wrestling

10) Andre Agassi and Rafael Nadal

Quiz 19

1) Who was the first person to swim 100 meters in under one minute?

2) What year was the first Formula One World Drivers' Championship?

3) What is the oldest championship in North American professional sports?

4) Cathy Rigby was the first woman to do what for *Sports Illustrated*?

5) What is the maximum number of dogs a musher can have on their team at the start of the Iditarod sled dog race?

6) What country had the most consecutive Davis Cup tennis finals appearances?

7) Who is the youngest jockey ever to win horse racing's Triple Crown?

8) Who was the first boxer to win the *Sports Illustrated* Sportsperson of the Year?

9) Who was the last amateur tennis player to win the U.S. Open?

10) How many fillies have won the Kentucky Derby?

Quiz 19 Answers

1) Johnny Weismuller – 58.6 seconds in the 100 meters freestyle in 1922
2) 1950
3) Stanley Cup – 1893
4) Pose nude
5) 16
6) Australia – 23 from 1946–1968
7) Steve Cauthen - He was 18 years old when he won the Triple Crown aboard Affirmed in 1978.
8) Ingemar Johansson - 1959
9) Arthur Ashe – 1968
10) Three – 1915, 1980, 1988

Quiz 20

1) What is the lowest score ever recorded for an 18-hole round of golf in a women's LPGA tournament?
2) Who is the youngest man to ever win a tennis grand slam singles title?
3) In the post 1968 open era, who was the first woman to win a calendar year tennis Grand Slam?
4) What father and son drivers were both Formula One World Champions?
5) How many male golfers have held all four major championships at the same time?
6) What female alpine skier has the most overall World Cup titles?
7) In 1954, world champion pool player Willie Mosconi set a record for consecutive shots without a miss in an exhibition; how many balls did he run without missing?
8) In what sport does a player use a cesta to hurl a pelota?
9) Who is the only person to hit an MLB home run and score an NFL touchdown in the same week?
10) Who are the only two women to win all four tennis Grand Slam singles tournaments during their career plus the Olympic singles gold medal?

Quiz 20 Answers

1) 59 - Annika Sorenstam in 2001

2) Michael Chang - 17 years, 110 days old when he won the 1989 French Open

3) Margaret Court - 1970

4) Graham and Damon Hill - Graham in 1962 and 1968 and son Damon in 1996

5) Two - Bobby Jones and Tiger Woods

6) Annmarie Moser-Proll (Austria) - six

7) 526

8) Jai-alai

9) Deion Sanders - September 1989

10) Steffi Graf and Serena Williams

Quiz 21

1) What driver has the most consecutive NASCAR championships?

2) Who was the first American born golfer to win the British Open?

3) What is the name of the biennial women's golf competition between teams from Europe and the United States?

4) Who is the only person to be named a first team high school All-American in football, basketball, and baseball?

5) How many male golfers have completed a double career Grand Slam by winning each of the four major championships at least twice?

6) Including the pre-1968 tennis era when only amateurs could compete, who was the first man to win a calendar year tennis Grand Slam?

7) What was the first U.S. men's professional sport to have female referees for regular season play?

8) Who was the first golfer to win the *Sports Illustrated* Sportsperson of the Year?

9) In 1930, who won the first Sullivan Award given to the most outstanding U.S. amateur athlete?

10) Who was the first African American to be named Associated Press female athlete of the year?

Quiz 21 Answers

1) Jimmie Johnson – five from 2006–2010
2) Walter Hagen – 1922
3) Solheim Cup – first played in 1990
4) Danny Ainge – He went to high school in Eugene, Oregon and won two NBA championships with the Boston Celtics and played MLB with the Toronto Blue Jays.
5) Two – Jack Nicklaus and Tiger Woods
6) Don Budge – 1938
7) NBA – 1997
8) Arnold Palmer – 1960
9) Bobby Jones – golf
10) Althea Gibson – tennis in 1957

Quiz 22

1) Who was the first female jockey to win a Triple Crown race?
2) How many tournaments have left handed female golfers won in LPGA history?
3) Who won the 2014 women's rugby World Cup?
4) Who was the first African American after Arthur Ashe to win a Wimbledon singles title?
5) What does NASCAR stand for?
6) What is the world's oldest golf course?
7) Who is the youngest man to win the Wimbledon tennis singles title?
8) What NASCAR driver has the most career victories?
9) What piece of sporting equipment has a maximum length of 42 inches and a maximum diameter of 2.61 inches?
10) In what was dubbed as "The Match of the Century", Seabiscuit defeated what 1937 Triple Crown winner in a 1938 match race?

Quiz 22 Answers

1) Julie Krone – 1993 Belmont Stakes aboard Colonial Affair
2) One – Bonnie Bryant in 1974

3) England
4) Venus Williams – 2000
5) National Association for Stock Car Automobile Racing
6) St. Andrews, Scotland – early 15th century
7) Boris Becker – 17 years old in 1985
8) Richard Petty – 200 wins
9) Baseball bat
10) War Admiral

Quiz 23

1) What country won the most consecutive Davis Cup tennis titles?
2) Who was the first female athlete to win 10 career gold medals in the IAAF World Track and Field Championships?
3) What golfer has the most PGA tour victories?
4) How many seconds must a cowboy stay aboard a rodeo bronc?
5) What is the largest population city in the U.S. that doesn't have an MLB, NFL, NBA, or NHL team?
6) Who was the first cyclist to win the *Sports Illustrated* Sportsperson of the Year?
7) Who is the first tennis player to win all four Grand Slam tournaments and an Olympic gold medal in tennis in the same calendar year?
8) Who has won the most heavyweight boxing title fights in history?
9) What year was the first men's soccer World Cup?
10) What male alpine skier has the most World Cup race wins?

Quiz 23 Answers

1) United States – seven from 1920–1926
2) Allyson Felix – U.S.
3) Sam Snead – 82 wins from 1936–1965
4) Eight
5) Austin, Texas – 11th largest city in U.S.
6) Greg LeMond – 1989
7) Steffi Graf – 1988

8) Joe Louis – He successfully defended his title 25 times.

9) 1930

10) Ingemar Stenmark (Sweden) - 86 wins from 1973–1989

Quiz 24

1) Based on number of participants, soccer is the most popular sport in the world; what is the second most popular sport?

2) Who is the only male golfer to complete a calendar year Grand Slam?

3) Who won the 2018 men's soccer World Cup?

4) In bowling, what is three strikes in a row called?

5) What driver has won the most Formula One World Championships?

6) What is the captain of a curling team called?

7) Who broke Bob Beamon's 1968 world long jump record?

8) Who won the first men's field hockey World Cup?

9) Counting both teams, how many players are on the field at one time in a men's field lacrosse game?

10) The actor who played Jethro Bodine on television's *The Beverly Hillbillies* was the son of a famous athlete; who was his father?

Quiz 24 Answers

1) Badminton – followed by field hockey

2) Bobby Jones – 1930

3) France

4) A turkey - In the late 18th and early 19th century, bowling tournaments gave out food items as tournament prizes and getting three strikes in a row became associated with winning a turkey and the name spread and stuck. Due to the much cruder equipment and lanes of long ago, getting three strikes in a row was a very difficult feat compared to today.

5) Michael Schumacher (Germany) - seven from 1994–2004

6) Skip

7) Mike Powell - 29 feet 4 3/8 inches in 1991

8) Pakistan - 1971

9) 20

10) Max Baer Sr. – world heavyweight boxing champion in 1934

Quiz 25

1) Who was the first male alpine skier to win three consecutive overall World Cup titles?

2) When Roger Bannister ran the first sub-four-minute mile, how long did his record stand?

3) Based on global following, soccer is the most popular sport in the world, what is the second most popular?

4) What NASCAR driver had the most victories from 1970-1979?

5) Giacomo Agostini won 122 Grand Prix and 15 world titles in what sport?

6) In what sport are you banned from playing left handed?

7) What sport originated the term home run?

8) Including the pre-1968 amateur only era, who was the first woman to win a calendar year tennis Grand Slam?

9) Who was the first American driver to win the Formula One World Championship?

10) How many golf major championships did Jack Nicklaus win?

Quiz 25 Answers

1) Gustav Thoni (Italy) – 1971-1973

2) 46 days

3) Cricket – followed by field hockey

4) Richard Petty – 89

5) Motorcycle racing

6) Polo - If a left-handed and right-handed player went for the ball, they would collide.

7) Cricket

8) Maureen Connolly – 1953

9) Phil Hill – 1961

10) 18

Quiz 26

1) The Fed Cup is the women's equivalent of the Davis Cup for men;

what country has won the most consecutive Fed Cup titles?

2) What is the name of competition between amateur golfers from the United States and Great Britain and Ireland?

3) Who golfer has the most LGPA tour wins in a single year?

4) Who was the last filly to win the Kentucky Derby?

5) What sport takes place in a 4.55-meter diameter circle?

6) Who won the first women's field hockey World Cup?

7) Who is the only driver to win five consecutive Formula One World Championships?

8) Who is the youngest woman to ever win a tennis grand slam singles title?

9) What female alpine skier has won the most consecutive overall World Cup titles?

10) Who has the most career Daytona 500 victories?

Quiz 26 Answers

1) United States - seven from 1976-1982

2) Walker Cup - established in 1922

3) Mickey Wright - 13 wins in 1963

4) Winning Colors - 1988

5) Sumo wrestling

6) Netherlands - 1974

7) Michael Schumacher (Germany) - 2000 to 2004

8) Martina Hingis – 16 years, 177 days old when she won the 1997 Australian Open

9) Annmarie Moser-Proll (Austria) - Five from 1971-1975

10) Richard Petty - seven

Quiz 27

1) What do Indianapolis 500 winners traditionally drink in the winner's circle?

2) What is the first Grand Slam tennis tournament played in a calendar year?

3) What horse has the fastest times ever for the Kentucky Derby, Preakness, and Belmont?

4) What year was the first Indianapolis 500 race?

5) What NASCAR driver was the first to start in 1,000 sanctioned races?

6) What single sporting event has the most in person spectators in the world?

7) Who won the 2010 men's soccer World Cup?

8) Who was the first professional bowler to win over $1 million in the PBA?

9) How many feet wide is a regulation volleyball court?

10) What are the two categories of harness racing?

Quiz 27 Answers

1) Milk
2) Australian Open
3) Secretariat – 1973
4) 1911
5) Richard Petty
6) Tour de France bicycle race – 12 to 15 million spectators
7) Spain
8) Earl Anthony – 1982
9) 30 feet
10) Trotting and pacing

Quiz 28

1) What four horses have won the Triple Crown since Secretariat in 1973?

2) In the post 1968 open era, who was the first man to win a calendar year tennis Grand Slam?

3) In cricket, how many runs are scored if the ball is hit over the boundary without bouncing?

4) What NASCAR driver had the most victories from 1980–1989?

5) Who won the 2015 women's soccer World Cup?

6) What golfer has the most career LPGA tour wins?

7) Who is the only jockey to win the *Sports Illustrated* Sportsperson of the Year?

8) Lacrosse was invented in what country?

9) What is the oldest stroke in competitive swimming?

10) What was the first country to win two consecutive women's rugby World Cups?

Quiz 28 Answers

1) Seattle Slew (1977), Affirmed (1978), American Pharoah (2015), Justify (2018)

2) Rod Laver – 1969

3) Six

4) Darrell Waltrip – 57

5) United States

6) Kathy Whitworth – 88 wins

7) Steve Cauthen – 1977

8) United States - Native Americans invented the game.

9) Breaststroke

10) New Zealand – 1998 and 2002

Quiz 29

1) Who is the only person to ever play in the Super Bowl and World Series?

2) When Affirmed won horse racing's Triple Crown in 1978, what horse finished second in each race?

3) What female alpine skier has the most World Cup race wins?

4) In 1457, King James II of Scotland banned what two sports because they interfered with archery practice needed for national defense?

5) What sport is played 11 on a side on ice with a ball?

6) According to USGA rules, how many clubs can a golfer have in their bag?

7) What two cities usually mark the end points of English Channel swims?

8) In golf, what device is used to measure the speed of the greens?

9) What sport features the fastest moving ball?

10) Who is the only person named Associated Press athlete of the year in two different sports?

Quiz 29 Answers

1) Deion Sanders – He played in the 1992 World Series with the Atlanta Braves and won two Super Bowls in 1995 with the San Francisco 49ers and in 1996 with the Dallas Cowboys.

2) Alydar

3) Lindsey Vonn – U.S.

4) Golf and soccer

5) Bandy

6) 14

7) Calais and Dover

8) Stimpmeter

9) Jai-alai – up to 188 mph

10) Babe Didrikson – track and field in 1932; golf in 1945, 1946, 1947, 1950, 1954

Baseball

Quiz 1

1) Who was the first Cincinnati Reds player to hit 50 home runs?
2) Who was the first manager to win the World Series with teams in both leagues?
3) What pitcher holds the record for most complete games?
4) What was the first MLB team to lose four World Series?
5) In 2001 for the first time in 100 years, what pitcher threw a shutout and hit a home run in his first MLB game?
6) Who were the first players ever selected season co-MVPs?
7) Who set a record playing 22 consecutive seasons at second base?
8) Who was the first pitcher to win a Cy Young Award in both leagues?
9) Of the 16 MLB franchises that were in place when the first World Series was played in 1903, how many have won the World Series?
10) How wide is the home plate?

Quiz 1 Answers

1) George Foster – 1977
2) Sparky Anderson – Cincinnati Reds (1975 and 1976) and Detroit Tigers (1984)
3) Cy Young – 749
4) New York Giants – After winning the second World Series in 1905, they lost for the fourth time in 1917.
5) Jason Jennings – Colorado Rockies
6) Willie Stargell and Keith Hernandez – 1977
7) Joe Morgan
8) Gaylord Perry – 1978
9) 16
10) 17 inches

Quiz 2

1) In 1959, an American League batter hit four home runs in one

game, how many years was it until another American League batter did it?

2) What player has appeared in the World Series with the largest number of teams?

3) What is the MLB record for most strikeouts by a pitcher in a nine-inning game?

4) Who was the first pitcher to win five Cy Young Awards?

5) What MLB team has the record for most consecutive seasons under .500?

6) How many times did Hank Aaron lead the league in home runs?

7) What player has the career record for most total bases?

8) Which MLB team had the most regular season wins from 1960-1969?

9) What is the record for most wins in a season by a pitcher?

10) Who was the first player with 3,000 hits and 500 home runs in their career?

Quiz 2 Answers

1) 43 years – 1959 to 2002
2) Lonnie Smith – four teams (Philadelphia, St. Louis, Kansas City, Atlanta)
3) 20
4) Roger Clemens
5) Pittsburgh Pirates – 20 years from 1993-2012
6) Four – 1957, 1963, 1966, 1967
7) Hank Aaron – 6,856
8) Baltimore Orioles (911–698)
9) 59 – Old Hoss Radbourn in 1884
10) Willie Mays – 1970

Quiz 3

1) Who is the only MLB player to hit a home run in every inning from the first to the sixteenth in their career?

2) Who was the first person to get over 1,400 extra base hits?

3) Who has the most consecutive seasons leading their league in

number of hits?

4) Who was the first person to steal 1,000 bases?

5) Who was the first player in MLB history to hit 50 home runs in a season?

6) Who pitched the only no-hit game in World Series history?

7) Who was the first rookie player to ever win a Gold Glove?

8) Who was the first American League switch hitter to hit for the cycle?

9) How many years did Babe Ruth's 60 home runs in a season record last?

10) Who has the most career batting titles?

Quiz 3 Answers

1) Willie Mays

2) Hank Aaron - 1,477 with 624 doubles, 98 triples, and 755 home runs

3) Ichiro Suzuki - five seasons from 2006-2010

4) Rickey Henderson

5) Babe Ruth - 1920

6) Don Larsen – 1956

7) Ken Hubbs - 1962 Chicago Cubs

8) Mickey Mantle - 1957

9) 34 years - 1927 to 1961

10) Ty Cobb – 11

Quiz 4

1) What was the first MLB franchise to move to three different states during their history?

2) Who was the first player to ever win three MLB MVP awards?

3) What pitcher led his league the most times in strikeouts?

4) Who was the first MLB catcher to have 400 career home runs?

5) In 1965, Satchell Paige pitched three innings for the Kansas City Athletics against the Boston Red Sox; how old was Paige?

6) Who was the first MLB switch-hitter to win multiple batting titles?

7) Who was the first MLB pitcher to reach 20 wins in a season with only one loss?

8) What is the record for most consecutive World Series titles?

9) Which MLB team had the most regular season wins from 1920-1929?

10) What year did Roger Maris hit 61 home runs?

Quiz 4 Answers

1) Baltimore Orioles - formerly Milwaukee Brewers (1901), St. Louis Browns (1902) and then Baltimore Orioles (1954)

2) Jimmie Foxx - 1932, 1933, 1938

3) Walter Johnson - 12 times

4) Mike Piazza

5) 59

6) Pete Rose - 1968, 1969, 1973

7) Roger Clemens - ended the season 20-3 in 2001

8) Five - New York Yankees from 1949-1953

9) New York Yankees (933-602)

10) 1961

Quiz 5

1) Who was the first player to hit 500 home runs and steal 500 bases?

2) Who was the first player to win two MVP awards?

3) Who holds the record with seven MVP Awards?

4) What is the record for the fewest pitches ever for a complete game?

5) Who was the first New York Yankee in history with 3,000 career hits?

6) From 1949 to 1964, how many World Series did the New York Yankees appear in?

7) What team did Ty Cobb end his career with?

8) How many years did Roger Maris' 61 home runs in a season record last?

9) What deaf-mute player inspired the non-verbal signs used in baseball and stole over 600 bases in his career?

10) Which MLB team had the most regular season wins from 1930-

1939?

Quiz 5 Answers

1) Barry Bonds – 2003
2) Walter Johnson – 1913 and 1924
3) Barry Bonds
4) 58 – by Charles Barrett in 1944
5) Derek Jeter – 2011
6) 14
7) Philadelphia Athletics – 1928
8) 37 years – 1961 to 1998
9) William Hoy – started his career in 1888
10) New York Yankees (970–554)

Quiz 6

1) What year did the American League first use the designated hitter rule?
2) Who was the first batter to strike out 2,000 times in their career?
3) Who was the first player named to 20 All-Star rosters?
4) What catcher had the most World Series appearances?
5) Who was the second player to hit 50 home runs in a season?
6) Which MLB team had the most regular season wins from 1980–1989?
7) In 1996, who was the first shortstop in 52 years to win an MLB batting title?
8) Who was the first pitcher in MLB history to throw four no hitters?
9) What was the first year that two players each hit four home runs in a game in the same league?
10) When the Chicago Cubs won the World Series in 2016, how many years had it been since their prior World Series win?

Quiz 6 Answers

1) 1973
2) Reggie Jackson

3) Stan Musial – 1963

4) Yogi Berra – 14 World Series appearances from 1947–1963 with the New York Yankees

5) Hack Wilson – 1930

6) New York Yankees (854-708)

7) Alex Rodriquez

8) Sandy Koufax – 1965

9) 2017 – Scooter Gennett and J.D. Martinez

10) 108 years – 1908

Quiz 7

1) What year was the first MLB domed stadium in operation?

2) Who has the most career World Series RBIs?

3) What Hall of Fame player won the batting Triple Crown with only nine home runs?

4) What is the highest MLB season batting average ever recorded?

5) Who was the first American League batter to hit four home runs in one game?

6) How many players have won more than one batting Triple Crown?

7) With a minimum of 3,000 plate appearances, who are the only three players ever with career batting averages over .350?

8) What American League team was the first to top 4 million attendance in a season?

9) What right handed batter has the most career strikeouts?

10) Who holds the American League record for most home runs in a season?

Quiz 7 Answers

1) 1965 – Houston Astrodome

2) Mickey Mantle – 40

3) Ty Cobb – 1909

4) .440 – Hugh Duffy in 1894

5) Lou Gehrig – 1932

6) Two – Rogers Hornsby and Ted Williams each won two.

7) Ty Cobb (.366), Rogers Hornsby (.359), Shoeless Joe Jackson (.356)

8) Toronto Blue Jays – 1993

9) Sammy Sosa – 2,306

10) Roger Maris – His 61 home runs in 1961 is still the American League record.

Quiz 8

1) Who holds the MLB record for most home runs in a season by a rookie?

2) In the live ball era from 1920 to present, three pitchers are tied for most wins in a season at 31; who are they?

3) Who was the first player to have a home run as their 3,000th hit?

4) Nolan Ryan has the post 1920 season strikeout record at 383; what is the all-time record?

5) Who became the oldest MLB rookie at age 42?

6) What was the first year that the American and National Leagues were split into divisions?

7) Who was the first pitcher with 100 strikeouts for 20 consecutive seasons?

8) In the post 1920 era, who has the most consecutive batting titles leading both leagues?

9) Who holds the MLB record reaching base in 84 consecutive games?

10) Which MLB team had the most regular season wins from 1940-1949?

Quiz 8 Answers

1) Aaron Judge – 52 in 2017

2) Jim Bagby Sr. (1921), Lefty Grove (1931), Denny McLain (1968)

3) Wade Boggs – 1999

4) 513 – Matt Kilroy in 1886

5) Satchel Paige

6) 1969

7) Don Sutton – 1985

8) Rod Carew – three from 1973-1975

9) Ted Williams – 1949

10) St. Louis Cardinals (960–580)

Quiz 9

1) What player has the highest on-base percentage ever?

2) Who is the only player who has won an MVP with two different teams in two different positions?

3) Who was the first person to win two batting Triple Crowns?

4) Who was the first relief pitcher to win a Cy Young Award in 1974?

5) In the live ball era from 1920 to present, what pitcher has the most shutouts in a season?

6) Who was the first rookie to lead the American League in RBIs?

7) What was the site of the first regular season game outside of the U.S.?

8) In 1994, Pete Rose broke the most games played record; whose record did he break?

9) Who was the first MLB African American player to win a batting title?

10) Who was the first player in MLB history to steal 100 bases in a season?

Quiz 9 Answers

1) Ted Williams - .482

2) Alex Rodriguez – Texas Rangers at shortstop and New York Yankees at third base

3) Rogers Hornsby - 1922 and 1925

4) Mike Marshall - Los Angeles Dodgers

5) Bob Gibson - 13 in 1968

6) Ted Williams - 145 in 1939

7) Montreal - 1969

8) Carl Yastrzemski

9) Jackie Robinson - 1949

10) Maury Wills – 1962

Quiz 10

1) Who has the most career World Series at bats?

2) Who is the first MLB player to have three games with three homes runs in the same season?

3) How many MLB players have had consecutive game hitting streaks of 40 or more games?

4) Who was the first pitcher to give up 500 home runs in their career?

5) Who was the first Philadelphia Phillies pitcher with 300 strikeouts in a season?

6) What player has won the most Gold Gloves?

7) Who is the only MLB player to hit a walk-off inside-the-park grand slam?

8) What U.S. president was the first to ever attend an MLB night game?

9) Who was the first black American League batting champion?

10) Who was the first person to win American League MVP and Rookie of the Year Awards in the same season?

Quiz 10 Answers

1) Yogi Berra – 259

2) Sammy Sosa – 2001

3) Five – Ty Cobb (40 in 1911), George Sisler (41 in 1922), Bill Dahlen (42 in 1894), Pete Rose (44 in 1978), Joe DiMaggio (56 in 1941)

4) Robin Roberts – 1966

5) Steve Carlton – 1972

6) Gregg Maddux – 18

7) Roberto Clemente – 1956

8) Harry Truman – 1946

9) Tony Oliva – 1964

10) Fred Lynn – 1975 with Boston Red Sox

Quiz 11

1) As player or manager, who was the first person to wear all four (Dodgers, Giants, Yankees, Mets) New York franchise uniforms?

2) In 2000, what did the Cincinnati Reds do for the first time in baseball's 162 game season history?

3) Who was the first manager to win the Manager of the Year Award

in both leagues?

4) Who was the first pitcher to have a no hitter in four consecutive seasons?

5) There have only been batting Triple Crown winners in consecutive years twice; what years was the last time this occurred?

6) Who was the first pitcher to need more than 20 seasons to get 300 wins?

7) In 1927 when Babe Ruth hit 60 home runs, who won the MVP Award?

8) Who was the first MLB player to steal home twice in one game?

9) Who was the first rookie to start in an MLB All-Star game?

10) What batter holds the record for being walked the most times in a season?

Quiz 11 Answers

1) Casey Stengel – player with Dodgers and Giants, manager with Yankees and Mets

2) They went the entire season without being shutout.

3) Bobby Cox – Toronto Blue Jays in 1985 and Atlanta Braves in 1991

4) Sandy Koufax – 1962 to 1965

5) 1966 and 1967 – Frank Robinson and Carl Yastrzemski

6) Don Sutton –1986

7) Lou Gehrig

8) Honus Wagner – 1901

9) Joe DiMaggio – 1936

10) Barry Bonds – 232 in 2004

Quiz 12

1) Who are the only two players who have five seasons with at least 30 home runs and 30 stolen bases?

2) Who was the first batter to strike out 200 times in a season?

3) What Cleveland player batted .408 for the season and was still runner up for the batting title?

4) Who has the most career at bats?

5) What is the record for most games lost by a pitcher in a season?

6) What pitcher has the career record for most wins?

7) Who has the most career World Series home runs?

8) Who was the first MLB catcher to have 200 hits in a season?

9) Who has the most career World Series runs scored?

10) Who has the MLB record for most total bases in a season?

Quiz 12 Answers

1) Bobby Bonds and Barry Bonds – father and son

2) Mark Reynolds – 204 times with the Arizona Diamondbacks in 2008

3) Shoeless Joe Jackson – 1911

4) Pete Rose – 14,555

5) 48 – John Coleman went 12–48 in his rookie season in 1883.

6) Cy Young – 511 wins

7) Mickey Mantle – 18

8) Mike Piazza – 201 hits for the 1997 Los Angeles Dodgers

9) Mickey Mantle – 42

10) Babe Ruth – 457 in 1921

Quiz 13

1) What team did Hank Aaron end his career with?

2) In 2000, the first MLB regular season game played outside of North America was played in what country?

3) Who was the first person to win a Cy Young and MVP Award in the same season?

4) How many Cy Young Awards did career strikeout leader Nolan Ryan win?

5) How old was the youngest player in MLB history?

6) What is the MLB record for most home runs by a team in a nine-inning game?

7) How many times did Babe Ruth hit four home runs in one game?

8) When Mark McGwire broke Roger Maris' season home run record, whose National League season home run record did he also break?

9) Who was the first baseball player to win the ESPY award for best male athlete?

10) In what year was the first MLB night game?

Quiz 13 Answers

1) Milwaukee Brewers
2) Japan – New York Mets and Chicago Cubs
3) Don Newcombe – 1956 Dodgers
4) None – He was runner-up once in 1973.
5) 15 – Joe Nuxhall for 1944 Cincinnati Reds
6) 10 – Toronto Blue Jays in 1987
7) Zero
8) Hack Wilson – 56 in 1930
9) Barry Bonds – 1994
10) 1935 – Philadelphia at Cincinnati

Quiz 14

1) Who was the first player to lead off four consecutive MLB games with a home run?
2) Who was the first player to win the MVP Award with two different teams?
3) During the 20th century, which MLB team had the most seasons with 100 or more wins?
4) Who was the first MLB pitcher ever with 800 starts?
5) Which MLB team had the most regular season wins from 1900–1909?
6) How many sets of brothers have pitched against each other in MLB games?
7) What year was the first MLB All-Star Game?
8) Who was the first MLB player with 300 home runs and 300 stolen bases in their career?
9) With a minimum of 3,000 plate appearances, who has the highest MLB career batting average?
10) Who had 14 World Series appearances and was season MVP three times?

Quiz 14 Answers

1) Brady Anderson – 1996
2) Rogers Hornsby – 1925 with the St. Louis Cardinals and 1929 with the Chicago Cubs
3) New York Yankees – 16
4) Cy Young
5) Chicago Cubs (693–362)
6) Eight – Jesse and Virgil Barnes, Joe and Phi Niekro, Gaylord and Jim Perry, Pat and Tom Underwood, Greg and Mike Maddux, Pedro and Ramon Martinez, Alan and Andy Benes, Jered and Jeff Weaver
7) 1933
8) Willie Mays – 1969
9) Ty Cobb – .366 over 24 seasons
10) Yogi Berra

Quiz 15

1) How old was the youngest player to appear in a World Series?
2) What two MLB players hold the record for playing the most consecutive seasons with the same team?
3) Who was the first player in MLB history to hit two grand slams in a game?
4) What MLB team holds the record for most home runs in a season?
5) What was Babe Ruth's first name?
6) Who was the first National League pitcher to strike out 20 batters in a game?
7) Who has the most career World Series hits?
8) What MLB player hit a home run from both sides of the plate in the same game 10 times over their career?
9) Babe Ruth was the first player to hit 50 or more home runs in a season four times; who was the second?
10) What MLB pitcher has the most career shutouts?

Quiz 15 Answers

1) 18 – Fred Lindstrom for the New York Giants in 1924

2) Brooks Robinson (Baltimore Orioles) and Carl Yastrzemski (Boston Red Sox) – 23 seasons

3) Tony Lazzeri – 1936 Yankees

4) Seattle Mariners – 264 in 1997

5) George

6) Kerry Wood – 1998

7) Yogi Berra – 71

8) Mickey Mantle

9) Mark McGwire – 1996 to 1999

10) Walter Johnson – 110

Quiz 16

1) Who has the MLB record for most steals of home?

2) Who was the second player to hit 50 home runs more than once for the same team?

3) How many stitches are on a regulation baseball?

4) Who was the last player to get a batting Triple Crown in the 20th century?

5) Who was the first Boston Red Sox player to hit 50 home runs in a season?

6) How many times did Willie Mays lead the league in home runs?

7) Who was the first MLB player to hit 50 home runs more than once for the same team?

8) What MLB player got two hits for two different teams in two different cities on the same day?

9) What two MLB teams played their first regular season games in 1977?

10) Who was the first person to have their jersey number retired from three different MLB teams?

Quiz 16 Answers

1) Ty Cobb – 54

2) Ralph Kiner – 1947 and 1949

3) 108

4) Carl Yastrzemski – 1967

5) Jimmie Foxx – 1938

6) Four – 1955, 1962, 1964, 1965

7) Babe Ruth – 1920 and 1921

8) Joel Youngblood – He was traded from the Mets to the Expos on August 4, 1982; after the Mets game day, he flew to Philadelphia which was hosting the Expos for a night game.

9) Seattle Mariners and Toronto Blue Jays

10) Nolan Ryan – Los Angeles Angels, Houston Astros, Texas Rangers

Quiz 17

1) Who has the MLB record for most run scored in a season?

2) Who was the first National League switch-hitter to win a batting title?

3) What jersey number did Jackie Robinson wear?

4) How many games long was Joe DiMaggio's MLB consecutive game hit streak record?

5) What is the only year in MLB history that there were batting Triple Crown winners in both leagues?

6) Since Ted Williams .400 season, what player has had the highest season batting average?

7) Who has the most consecutive years leading their league in stolen bases?

8) In Joe DiMaggio's record consecutive game hit streak, how many times did he get only one hit?

9) In 2001, Barry Bonds set a record for being walked 177 times in a season; whose record did he break?

10) Which MLB team had the most regular season wins from 2000-2009?

Quiz 17 Answers

1) Babe Ruth – 179 in 1921

2) Pete Rose – 1968

3) 42

4) 56

5) 1933 – Jimmie Foxx (AL) and Chuck Klein (NL)

6) Tony Gwynn – .394 with San Diego in 1994

7) Luis Aparicio – nine from 1956-1964

8) 34 times

9) Babe Ruth – 170 walks in 1923

10) New York Yankees (965-651)

Quiz 18

1) What MLB team has the record for most consecutive seasons above .500?

2) Who was the first U.S. president to throw out a first pitch at an MLB game?

3) How did the Los Angeles Dodgers get their team name?

4) Since Joe DiMaggio's record, who has the longest consecutive game streak with at least one hit?

5) Who was the first pitcher with 300 strikeouts in a season?

6) What was the first year that both MLB leagues had at least 10 teams?

7) Who was the last MLB pitcher to win 30 or more games in a season?

8) Who is the only player to steal home more than 50 times in their career?

9) Who was the first person to win four consecutive Cy Young Awards?

10) Ty Cobb held the record for being the youngest player ever to win a batting title for 48 years; who broke his record?

Quiz 18 Answers

1) New York Yankees – 39 years from 1926-1964

2) William Howard Taft – 1910

3) The team was established in Brooklyn in 1883 and went through various names before settling on the Trolley Dodgers which refers to the network of trolleys in Brooklyn which were a major cause of accidents at the time, so people were familiar with dodging trolleys. Over time, the name was shortened to Dodgers, and when the team moved to Los Angeles after the 1957 season, the name was kept.

4) Pete Rose – 44 games in 1978

5) Rube Waddell – 1903

6) 1962

7) Denny McLain – He had a 31-6 season with the 1968 Detroit Tigers.

8) Ty Cobb - 54 times

9) Gregg Maddux - 1992 to 1995

10) Al Kaline – He was 20 years old and one day younger than Cobb was when he won the title with the Detroit Tigers in 1955.

Quiz 19

1) What pitcher has the most career losses?

2) Pete Rose has the career record for most regular season games played; whose record did he break?

3) Who was the first pitcher to ger 3,000 career strikeouts?

4) Who is the only MLB player to win MVP in both leagues?

5) What MLB team has the highest season win percentage in history?

6) Who was the first player to hit four home runs in a World Series?

7) Who was the first MLB pitcher to strike out 4,000 batters?

8) What year did the National and American Leagues first both exist?

9) From 1920 on, what MLB pitcher has the most wins?

10) Who was the first player to hit 400 home runs and steal 400 bases?

Quiz 19 Answers

1) Cy Young – 316 losses

2) Carl Yastrzemski

3) Walter Johnson - 1923

4) Frank Robinson – 1961 with the Cincinnati Reds and 1966 with the Baltimore Orioles

5) Chicago Cubs - In 1906, the Cubs had a record of 116-36 for a winning percentage of .763.

6) Babe Ruth - 1926

7) Nolan Ryan

8) 1901

9) Warren Spahn - 363

10) Barry Bonds - 1998

Quiz 20

1) What pitcher has the most consecutive years leading their league in strikeouts?

2) Who was the first player to win consecutive league MVP awards?

3) What three pitchers have won three pitching Triple Crowns?

4) What is the MLB record for most games started in a season by a pitcher?

5) Who was the first pitcher to throw four no-hitters?

6) What player has been named to the most All-Star rosters ever?

7) Who was the first player to play 150 games in a season without getting at least 50 singles?

8) What National League player was the first to hit .400 for a season?

9) Who has the most career World Series base on balls?

10) Who was the first pitcher to strike out a side with nine pitches in both leagues?

Quiz 20 Answers

1) Walter Johnson - eight from 1912-1919

2) Jimmie Foxx - 1932, 1933

3) Grover Cleveland Alexander, Walter Johnson, Sandy Koufax

4) 75 - Will White in 1879 and Pud Galvin in 1883

5) Sandy Koufax - 1965

6) Hank Aaron - 21 times

7) Barry Bonds - In 2001, he had 49 singles and 73 home runs.

8) Ross Barnes - .429 in 1876

9) Mickey Mantle - 43

10) Nolan Ryan

Quiz 21

1) How many batting titles did Willie Mays win?

2) Which MLB team had the most regular season wins from 1950-1959?

3) What MLB team has the record for most consecutive years in the playoffs?

4) Who was the first pitcher with 300 saves?

5) Who was the first player to win a league MVP Award while on a last place team?

6) Who was the first MLB player to play in all four divisions in one season?

7) What MLB team has the record for most consecutive years out of the playoffs?

8) Who was the first MLB pitcher to strike out 300 batters in four consecutive seasons?

9) What was the first MLB team with four 30 home run hitters in the same season?

10) Who holds the MLB record for career strikeouts as a batter?

Quiz 21 Answers

1) One – 1954

2) New York Yankees (955–582)

3) New York Yankees – 13 years from 1995–2007

4) Rollie Fingers – 1982

5) Andre Dawson – 1987 Chicago Cubs

6) Dave Kingman – 1977

7) Baltimore Orioles – 41 years from 1903–1943

8) Randy Johnson – 1999 to 2002

9) Los Angeles Dodgers – Dusty Baker (30), Ron Cey (30), Steve Garvey (33), Reggie Smith (32)

10) Reggie Jackson – 2,597

Quiz 22

1) Who pitched in 1,252 MLB games over 24 years?

2) Who was the first player to hit 50 home runs in a season for two different teams?

3) Who was the first MLB rookie to steal at least 100 bases?

4) As a pitcher, how many seasons did Babe Ruth have 20 or more wins?

5) What was the only MLB season without a champion declared in either league?

6) Who has the most consecutive years leading their league in number of at bats?

7) Who held the MLB record for stolen bases in a season for 47 years?

8) What year did the Chicago Cubs play their first night game at Wrigley Field?

9) What year did the World Series begin?

10) Which MLB team had the most regular season wins from 1970–1979?

Quiz 22 Answers

1) Jesse Orosco – for the Mets, Dodgers, Indians, Brewers, Orioles, Cardinals, Padres, Yankees, and Twins

2) Jimmie Foxx – Philadelphia Athletics (1932) and Boston Red Sox (1938)

3) Vince Coleman – 1985

4) Two – 1916, 1917

5) 1994 – baseball strike

6) Ichiro Suzuki – five from 2004–2008

7) Ty Cobb – set in 1915

8) 1988

9) 1903

10) Cincinnati Reds (953–657)

Quiz 23

1) What player has the most World Series appearances?

2) In the modern two league era, what MLB team has the record for the longest losing streak?

3) Who was the first player to win three MVP Awards?

4) Who was the first catcher to win 10 Golden Gloves?

5) What two players are the first teammates to both have 30 home runs and 30 stolen bases in the same season?

6) Who has the MLB record for most career home runs by a pitcher?

7) Who was the first MLB pitcher to strike out the first seven batters they faced in a game?

8) What Hall of Fame player was on the cover of the very first *Sports*

Illustrated ever published in August 1954?

9) What MLB team was the first to put their names on the back of their jerseys?

10) What year did the first Canadian team win the World Series?

Quiz 23 Answers

1) Yogi Berra - 14
2) Philadelphia Phillies – 23 games in 1961
3) Jimmie Foxx – 1932, 1933, 1938
4) Johnny Bench - 10 consecutive from 1968-1977 with the Cincinnati Reds
5) Howard Johnson and Darryl Strawberry - 1987 New York Mets
6) Wes Ferrell - 38
7) Denny McLain – 1965
8) Eddie Mathews
9) Chicago White Sox - 1960
10) 1992 – Toronto Blue Jays

Quiz 24

1) How many MLB teams are named for birds?
2) Who has the highest career slugging percentage?
3) Who was the first pitcher to win the Cy Young Award without winning 20 or more games?
4) Who was the first MLB player with 3,000 hits?
5) What two MLB teams share the record for most wins in a season at 116?
6) Who is the only MLB player to hit 60 or more home runs in a season three times?
7) Who is the only MLB player to hit two grand slams in one inning?
8) What was the first year that two MLB players each hit four home runs in a game?
9) Who was the first player to win All-Star Game MVP and World Series MVP in the same year?
10) Who was the first National League player to hit 30 home runs in a season?

Quiz 24 Answers

1) Three – Cardinals, Orioles, Blue Jays
2) Babe Ruth - .690
3) Tom Seaver - He had a 19-10 record for the 1973 New York Mets.
4) Cap Anson - 1897
5) Chicago Cubs (1906 in a 154-game season) and Seattle Mariners (2001 in a 162-game season)
6) Sammy Sosa - in 1998, 1999, 2001
7) Fernando Tatis - April 23, 1999
8) 2002 - Mike Cameron (AL) and Shawn Green (NL)
9) Derek Jeter - 2000
10) Rogers Hornsby - 42 in 1922

Quiz 25

1) In the post 1920 era, who has the most consecutive batting titles?
2) What pitcher threw only three pitches in an inning to get three outs and did it four times in their career?
3) What year did the American League first require batting helmets?
4) Which MLB team had the most regular season wins from 1910-1919?
5) What MLB pitcher has the record for most consecutive scoreless innings?
6) How old was the oldest player to appear in a World Series?
7) What was the first team to win two World Series?
8) Who is the only pitcher in MLB history to throw consecutive no hitters?
9) How many consecutive games did Cal Ripken Jr. play in?
10) What National League team was the first to top 4 million attendance in a season?

Quiz 25 Answers

1) Rogers Hornsby - six from 1920-1925
2) Walter Johnson
3) 1957

4) San Francisco Giants (889–597)

5) Orel Hershiser – 59 innings

6) 46 - Jack Quinn from the Philadelphia Athletics in 1930

7) Chicago Cubs - 1907 and 1908

8) Johnny Vander Meer - 1938 Cincinnati Reds

9) 2,632 games – from 1982–1998

10) Colorado Rockies – 1993

Quiz 26

1) Who was the first MLB player to have a .400 batting average in two or more seasons?

2) Who has the most career World Series strikeouts as a batter?

3) Who was the first pitcher to win MVP in consecutive seasons?

4) Who was the first New York Mets pitcher to win 25 games?

5) Who was the first player to hit 50 or more home runs in four consecutive seasons?

6) Prior to the batting Triple Crown winner in 2012, how many years had it been since there was a batting Triple Crown winner?

7) What pitcher holds the MLB record for most no hitters?

8) What player has the most Gold Gloves for a third baseman and is tied for second most ever?

9) Who was the longest tenured MLB manager with a single team?

10) Which MLB team had the most regular season wins from 1990–1999?

Quiz 26 Answers

1) Ed Delahanty - 1894 and 1895

2) Mickey Mantle - 54

3) Hal Newhouser - Detroit Tigers in 1944 and 1945

4) Tom Seaver - 1969

5) Mark McGwire - 1996 to 1999

6) 45 years - Carl Yastrzemski in 1967

7) Nolan Ryan – seven

8) Brooks Robinson - 16

9) Connie Mack - with the Philadelphia Athletics from 1901-1950

10) Atlanta Braves (925-629)

Quiz 27

1) In 1931, what female pitcher became the first woman in professional baseball to strike out Babe Ruth and Lou Gehrig in an exhibition game?

2) What year did Hank Aaron break Babe Ruth's career home run record?

3) What year was Bobby Thompson's "Shot heard round the world" in the playoff game between the Dodgers and Giants?

4) Who has the highest season batting average ever for a starting pitcher?

5) Who was the first black MLB manager?

6) From 1920 on, what MLB pitcher has the most losses?

7) What MLB team set a consecutive game winning streak record in 2017?

8) What MLB pitcher has the most consecutive years leading their league in number of wins?

9) Who was the first MLB pitcher to play for 27 seasons?

10) In what year did the last MLB player bat .400?

Quiz 27 Answers

1) Jackie Mitchell - In an exhibition game between the New York Yankees and the Chattanooga Lookouts, who were a class AA minor league team, she struck out Ruth and Gehrig in succession; she was 17 years old at the time. Baseball commissioner Kenesaw Mountain Landis banned women from the sport later that year.

2) 1974

3) 1951

4) Walter Johnson - .433 in 1925

5) Frank Robinson – 1975 Cleveland Indians

6) Nolan Ryan – 292 losses

7) Cleveland Indians - 22 games

8) Warren Spahn - five from 1957-1961

9) Nolan Ryan – from 1966-1993

10) 1941 – Ted Williams

Quiz 28

1) Since 1920, what pitcher holds the record for most walks in a season?

2) What player has the most World Series wins?

3) In the post 1920 era, who has the highest season batting average ever?

4) Sandy Koufax broke the single season strikeout record with 382 in 1965; whose record did he break?

5) What year was the first batting helmet worn by an MLB team?

6) Who is the only pitcher with three Triple Crowns where they led both leagues?

7) Ichiro Suzuki broke the single season hits record with 262 in 2004; whose 84-year-old record did he break?

8) Who was the first MLB player to hit four home runs in one game?

9) When Nolan Ryan set the single season strikeout record in 1973, how much did he break the prior record by?

10) The St. Louis Cardinals' name didn't originally refer to the bird; what did it reference?

Quiz 28 Answers

1) Bob Feller – 208 in 1938

2) Yogi Berra – 10

3) Rogers Hornsby – .424 in 1924

4) Bob Feller – 348 in 1946

5) 1941 – Brooklyn Dodgers

6) Sandy Koufax – 1963, 1965, 1966

7) George Sisler – 257 hits in 1920

8) Bobby Lowe – 1894

9) One strikeout – He broke Sandy Koufax's record of 382.

10) The color of their uniforms – Willie McHale, a columnist for the St. Louis Republic, overheard a woman in the stands describe the uniforms as a shade of cardinal. He began using the nickname rather than their previous name, the Perfectos, and it caught on. The bird logo didn't appear until the 1920s.

Quiz 29

1) Who was the last person to win a batting Triple Crown?
2) Who was the first pitcher over age 40 with 300 strikeouts in a season?
3) Who has held the MLB season RBI record since 1930?
4) Who was the first MLB player in the 20th century to reach 3,000 hits?
5) Who is the only starting pitcher in a World Series game to bat other than ninth?
6) Who was the first MLB player to hit home runs in his teens and in his forties?
7) Who was the first southpaw pitcher to get 4,000 strikeouts?
8) Babe Ruth was the first player ever to lead their league in home runs at least eight times; who was the second?
9) What brothers were the first to face each other as rookie starting pitchers?
10) What two pitchers are the first teammates to both have 300 or more strikeouts in the same season?

Quiz 29 Answers

1) Miguel Cabrera – 2012
2) Nolan Ryan – 1989
3) Hack Wilson – 191 in 1930
4) Honus Wagner – 1914
5) Babe Ruth
6) Ty Cobb – He played from 1905–1928 and started in MLB at age 18.
7) Steve Carlton – 1986
8) Mike Schmidt
9) Greg and Mike Maddux – 1986
10) Randy Johnson and Curt Schilling – 2002 Arizona Diamondbacks

Basketball

Quiz 1

1) Who was the first NBA player with more than 15,000 assists?

2) UCLA's consecutive game winning streak from 1971–1974 was broken in a loss to what team?

3) Who was the first NBA player drafted number one who never played U.S. high school or college basketball?

4) Who holds the NBA record for most career fouls?

5) What is the NBA record for most consecutive free throws made?

6) Who has the highest NCAA men's career scoring average?

7) Who was the first player on a NCAA Division I men's basketball team to score 100 points in a single game?

8) Who was the first NBA player with 2,000 rebounds in a season?

9) Who holds the career record for most NBA games played?

10) Who was the first player to win three consecutive NBA MVP awards?

Quiz 1 Answers

1) John Stockton

2) Notre Dame – Notre Dame was also the last loss at the beginning of the streak.

3) Yao Ming

4) Kareem Abdul-Jabbar – 4,657

5) 97 – Michael Williams in 1993

6) Pete Maravich – 44.2 ppg for LSU from 1967–1970

7) Frank Selvy – He scored 100 points for Furman University against Newberry College in 1954.

8) Wilt Chamberlain – 1960–61

9) Robert Parish – 1,611

10) Bill Russell in 1960–61, 1961–62, 1962–63

Quiz 2

1) How many NCAA Division I men's teams have gone undefeated in winning the national championship?

2) Who was the first player to lead the NBA in scoring and assists in the same season?

3) Who holds the NBA career record for most games with 20 or more points?

4) Who is the oldest NBA player to score 50 points in a game?

5) Excluding Wilt Chamberlain, what NBA player has the highest season points per game average?

6) Who led the American Basketball Association (ABA) the most times in rebounding?

7) Who is the oldest player to lead the NBA in scoring?

8) Who are the only two NBA players with more than 50 rebounds in a game?

9) Who holds the NBA career record for most seasons leading the league in points?

10) What is the theme song of the Harlem Globetrotters?

Quiz 2 Answers

1) Seven – San Francisco (1956), North Carolina (1957), UCLA (1964), UCLA (1967), UCLA (1972), UCLA (1973), Indiana (1976)

2) Nate Archibald – 34 ppg and 11.4 assists in 1971–72

3) Karl Malone – 1,134

4) Michael Jordan – 38

5) Elgin Baylor – 38.3 ppg average for 1961–62 Los Angeles Lakers

6) Artis Gilmore – four times

7) Michael Jordan – 35

8) Bill Russell and Wilt Chamberlain

9) Michael Jordan – 11

10) Sweet Georgia Brown

Quiz 3

1) What year was the first WNBA season?

2) Excluding UCLA, what is the most consecutive years a school has appeared in the men's NCAA Division I Final Four?

3) What college team holds the record for the second most men's NCAA Division I basketball championships?

4) Who is the only coach to win both an NCAA Division I basketball championship and an NBA title?

5) Who was drafted number one in the 1984 NBA draft that Michael Jordan was part of?

6) Who was the first NBA player to get 300 steals in a season?

7) What school holds the record for most consecutive men's NCAA Division I final four appearances?

8) Who is the oldest NBA player to score 30 points in a game?

9) What school holds the record for most consecutive men's NCAA Division I tournament appearances?

10) How many feet wide is a regulation NBA court?

Quiz 3 Answers

1) 1997
2) Five years - Cincinnati (1959-1963), Duke (1988-1992)
3) Kentucky
4) Larry Brown – Kansas in 1988 and Detroit Pistons in 2004
5) Hakeem Olajuwon
6) Alvin Robertson - San Antonio Spurs in 1985-86
7) UCLA - 10 in a row from 1967-1976
8) Michael Jordan - 40
9) Kansas
10) 50 feet

Quiz 4

1) Who holds the career record for most consecutive NBA games played?

2) What Houston Rockets duo were known as the Twin Towers?

3) Who holds the NBA record for most career free throws made?

4) What NBA player scored the most points during the 1950s?

5) Who holds the NBA record for most consecutive games with at least

one steal?

6) What NBA team has the most regular season wins from 1990-1999?

7) Who is the oldest NBA player to score 20 points in a game?

8) Who was the first NBA player to score 2,000 points in a season?

9) Who is the only NBA player to average 30 points and 20 rebounds as a rookie?

10) What NBA player scored the most points during the 1970s?

Quiz 4 Answers

1) A.C. Greene - 1,192

2) Hakeem Olajuwon and Ralph Sampson

3) Karl Malone - 9,787

4) Dolph Schayes

5) Chris Paul - 108

6) Chicago Bulls (558-230)

7) Kareem Abdul-Jabbar - 41

8) George Yardley - Detroit Falcons in 1957-58

9) Wilt Chamberlain - 37.6 ppg and 27.0 rpg in 1959-60

10) Kareem Abdul-Jabbar

Quiz 5

1) Who won the NCAA Division I national championship the first year the tournament expanded to 64 teams?

2) What team won the most consecutive NBA championships?

3) How many times did Wilt Chamberlain score 50 or more points in an NBA game?

4) How many NBA titles did Magic Johnson win in his career?

5) What year did the NBA adopt the three-point shot?

6) Who holds the NBA career record for most turnovers?

7) Who has the most career NBA MVP awards?

8) What is the fewest number of losses by an NBA team in an 82-game season?

9) According to NBA rules, how long does a player have to shoot a free throw after catching the ball?

10) Who holds the NBA career record for most minutes played?

Quiz 5 Answers

1) Villanova
2) Boston Celtics – eight from 1959–1966
3) 118
4) Five – 1980, 1982, 1985, 1987 1988
5) 1979
6) Karl Malone – 4,524
7) Kareem Abdul-Jabbar – six
8) Nine – Golden State Warriors in 2015-16
9) 10 seconds
10) Kareem Abdul-Jabbar – 57,446 minutes

Quiz 6

1) What year did the men's NCAA Division I tournament expand to 64 teams?
2) Who is the only player to start every game in four consecutive men's NCAA Division I final four appearances?
3) Who holds the NBA record for highest career rebounds per game?
4) What NBA player scored the most points during the 1960s?
5) What was Michael Jordan's number?
6) How many years did Michael Jordan lead the NBA in points?
7) What Hall of Fame player won four MVP awards and had a higher field goal average than free throw percentage over their career?
8) Who holds the NBA career record for most steals?
9) How many NBA finals MVP Awards did Michael Jordan win?
10) Who is the oldest NBA player to win league MVP?

Quiz 6 Answers

1) 1985
2) Christian Laettner – Duke 1989-1992
3) Wilt Chamberlain – 22.9 rpg
4) Wilt Chamberlain

5) 23

6) 11

7) Wilt Chamberlain – 54% field goal, 51% free throw

8) John Stockton – 3,265

9) Six

10) Karl Malone – 35

Quiz 7

1) How many points were scored in the highest scoring NBA regular season game ever?

2) What basketball player was the first non-American winner of the ESPY Award?

3) What college has won the most NCAA Division I women's titles?

4) How many players have ever won NCAA, Olympic, and NBA championships?

5) Who holds the NBA career record for most points?

6) Who was the first player in the WNBA to dunk?

7) What is the NBA record for most field goals made by a player in a game with no misses?

8) In one of the most famous shots in NCAA tournament history, who threw the inbounds pass to Christian Laettner to win the regional final in 1992?

9) Who is the only NBA player to record a double-triple-double (20 or more points, rebounds, and assists) in a game?

10) What four ABA teams joined the NBA when the two leagues merged?

Quiz 7 Answers

1) 370 – The Detroit Pistons beat the Denver Nuggets 186–184 in triple overtime in 1983.

2) Dirk Nowitzki – 2011

3) Connecticut

4) Seven – Clyde Lovellette, Bill Russell, K.C. Jones, Jerry Lucas, Quinn Buckner, Michael Jordan, Magic Johnson

5) Kareem Abdul-Jabbar – 38,387

6) Lisa Leslie – 2002

7) 18 – Wilt Chamberlain

8) Grant Hill

9) Wilt Chamberlain – 1968

10) New York Nets, Denver Nuggets, Indiana Pacers, San Antonio Spurs

Quiz 8

1) What player holds the record for most career points in the men's NCAA Division I tournament?

2) What NBA team had the most regular season wins from 1960–1969?

3) At the time of his retirement in 2005, who held the NBA record for most three-pointers made in a career?

4) What team won the most championships in the eight seasons of the American Basketball Association (ABA)?

5) Who is the only coach to win both an NBA and WNBA title?

6) Who is the only NBA player to win MVP, defensive player of the year, and finals MVP in the same year?

7) What NBA player had the longest career with one team?

8) What was the original name of the NBA?

9) Who is the career NCAA Division I men's scoring leader?

10) Excluding UCLA, what is the most consecutive years a school has appeared in the men's NCAA Division I championship game?

Quiz 8 Answers

1) Christian Laettner – 407 for Duke 1989-1992

2) Boston Celtics (571-228)

3) Reggie Miller

4) Indiana Pacers – three championships

5) Paul Westhead – Los Angeles Lakers (1980) and Phoenix Mercury (2007)

6) Hakeem Olajuwon – 1994

7) Dirk Nowitzki

8) BAA – Basketball Association of America until 1949

9) Pete Maravich – 3,667 points for LSU from 1967-1970

10) Three years - Cincinnati (1961-1963), Duke (1990-1992), Kentucky (1996-1998), Ohio State (1960-1962)

Quiz 9

1) Who led the NBA in rebounds per game for seven straight seasons in the 1990s?

2) Who holds the NBA career record for most seasons leading the league in field goal percentage?

3) How many scoring titles did Wilt Chamberlain win during his career?

4) In the 1961-62 season, Wilt Chamberlain led the NBA in minutes played per game; what was unusual about his minutes per game number?

5) Who was the first Utah Jazz player to win league MVP?

6) What college has won the most consecutive NCAA Division I women's titles?

7) Who holds the NBA record for most free throws attempted in a game with none made?

8) Who was the lone college player on the 1992 Olympic Dream Team?

9) Who was the first women's NCAA Division I tournament champion?

10) What is the NBA record for highest season points per game?

Quiz 9 Answers

1) Dennis Rodman

2) Shaquille O'Neal – 10 seasons

3) Seven

4) It was more than the minutes in a game. He played every minute of the 80-game season, and with overtime games ended up averaging 48.5 minutes played per game.

5) Karl Malone - 1996-97 season

6) Connecticut - four from 2013-2016

7) Shaquille O'Neal – 11

8) Christian Laettner

9) Louisiana Tech - 1982

10) 50.4 ppg - Wilt Chamberlain in 1961-62 season

Quiz 10

1) Who is the oldest NBA player with 20 rebounds in a game?

2) Who holds the NBA career record for most offensive rebounds?

3) What player holds the record for most career games won in the men's NCAA Division I tournament?

4) What two players share the NBA career record for most consecutive seasons leading the league in points?

5) Who is the only NBA player to record 40 points and 40 rebounds in a game?

6) Who had the NBA's first recorded quadruple double (double digit figures in four statistical categories) in a game?

7) What NBA player scored the most points during the 1980s?

8) Who were the members of Michigan's Fab Five team who as starting freshman made it to the 1992 NCAA championship game?

9) Who is credited with inventing basketball?

10) What is the only team that was part of the ABA for its entire nine years without ever moving or changing its name and then joined the NBA and still has not moved or changed its name?

Quiz 10 Answers

1) Dikembe Mutombo – 40 years old

2) Moses Malone – 6,731

3) Christian Laettner – 21 for Duke 1989–1992

4) Wilt Chamberlain and Michael Jordan – seven

5) Wilt Chamberlain – 1968

6) Nate Thurmond – 1974 Chicago Bulls with 22 points, 14 rebounds, 13 assists and 12 blocks in a game

7) Alex English

8) Ray Jackson, Jimmy King, Juwan Howard, Chris Webber, Jalen Rose

9) James Naismith

10) Indiana Pacers

Quiz 11

1) Who was the first NBA player to average a triple-double for a season?

2) Who is the oldest NBA player with 20 assists in a game?

3) What player holds the record for most career games played in the men's NCAA Division I tournament?

4) Who was the first lottery pick in NBA history?

5) In 1995, who surpassed Red Auerbach for career wins by a coach?

6) What team won the very first men's NCAA Division I National Championship?

7) What year was basketball invented?

8) Who is the oldest NBA player with 10 steals in a game?

9) Which team did Kareen Abdul-Jabbar begin his NBA career with?

10) Which NBA team set a record of 33 consecutive regular season wins in 1971-72?

Quiz 11 Answers

1) Oscar Robertson - 30.8 points, 12.5 rebounds and 11.4 assists in 1961-62

2) Steve Nash – 37 years old

3) Christian Laettner - 23 for Duke 1989-1992

4) Patrick Ewing - New York Knicks in 1985

5) Lanny Wilkens

6) Oregon Ducks - 1939

7) 1891

8) Jerry West – 35 years old

9) Milwaukee Bucks - six seasons

10) Los Angeles Lakers

Quiz 12

1) Who was the first NBA player to have 10 steals in a game?

2) Who was the most recent player to win NCAA, Olympic, and NBA championships?

3) What two-time NBA champion became a U.S. Senator and ran for U.S. President?

4) What is the NBA record for most points scored by a player in a half?

5) Who was the first WNBA three-time MVP?

6) How long was Connecticut's NCAA record women's consecutive game win streak which ended in 2017?

7) Who stunned Kentucky to win the national championship in one of the greatest NCAA tournament upsets ever in 1966?

8) Who is the oldest NBA player to score 40 points in a game?

9) Who holds the NBA career record for most defensive rebounds?

10) What is the NBA record for most consecutive 50 points games by a player?

Quiz 12 Answers

1) Jerry West – 1973

2) Magic Johnson – 1979 NCAA champion with Michigan State, first NBA championship in 1980 with Los Angeles Lakers, 1992 Olympic champion

3) Bill Bradley

4) 59 – Wilt Chamberlain in his 100-point game

5) Sheryl Swoopes – 2005

6) 111 games

7) Texas Western – first all African-American lineup to win a national championship

8) Michael Jordan – 40 years old

9) Kevin Garnett – 11,453

10) Seven – Wilt Chamberlain in 1961

Quiz 13

1) How long was UCLA's NCAA record men's consecutive game win streak which ended in 1974?

2) What year did the last undefeated team win the NCAA Division I basketball championship?

3) In terms of number of games, what NBA player is the second fastest to reach 20,000 points?

4) Who were the first two NBA teammates to both score 2,000 points in a season?

5) Who was the inaugural winner of the NBA three-point shootout in the 1985-86 season?

6) What school holds the record for most men's NCAA Division I

tournament appearances?

7) Who was the first NBA player with more than 3,000 steals?

8) What year was the first NBA Canadian team?

9) Who was one of the first dominant players in the NBA and won five championships and wore number 99?

10) What NBA team had the most regular season wins from 2000–2009?

Quiz 13 Answers

1) 88 games

2) 1976 – Indiana

3) Michael Jordan – 620 games

4) Jerry West and Elgin Baylor – Los Angeles Lakers 1964–65 season

5) Larry Bird

6) Kentucky

7) John Stockton

8) 1946 – The Toronto Huskies only lasted one season.

9) George Mikan – Minneapolis Lakers from 1947–1956

10) San Antonio Spurs (576–244)

Quiz 14

1) Who was the first woman ever selected in the NBA draft?

2) What NBA team had the most regular season wins from 1950–1959?

3) Who holds the NBA career record for most seasons leading the league in points per game?

4) Excluding UCLA, what is the most consecutive years a school has won the men's NCAA Division I championship?

5) What was the first year that the NCAA men's tournament had named regions?

6) Who led the American Basketball Association (ABA) the most times in scoring?

7) What school holds the record for most consecutive men's NCAA Division I basketball championships?

8) What was the winningest team in the eight seasons of the American Basketball Association (ABA)?

9) What player won 11 NBA championships and five MVP awards?

10) Who holds the NBA career record for most blocks?

Quiz 14 Answers

1) Lucy Harris - She never actually played but was selected in 1977 by the New Orleans Jazz.

2) Boston Celtics (408-298)

3) Michael Jordan - 10

4) Two years - Oklahoma State (1945-1946), Kentucky (1948-1949), San Francisco (1955-1956), Cincinnati (1961-1962), Duke (1991-1992), Florida (2006-2007)

5) 1956 - Th final four structure had been around since 1952, but the regions weren't named.

6) Julius Erving - three times

7) UCLA - seven

8) Kentucky Colonels (448-296)

9) Bill Russell

10) Hakeem Olajuwon - 3,830

Quiz 15

1) Who was the second NBA player ever to average a triple-double over a season?

2) How many consecutive seasons did John Stockton lead the NBA in assists per game?

3) What was the first year the NBA used a 24 second shot clock?

4) What year did the University of Connecticut win both the men's and women's NCAA Division I basketball championships?

5) In 1984, Georgetown with Patrick Ewing won their first national championship; who did they beat in the final?

6) How many times was Lew Alcindor named outstanding player in the NCAA tournament?

7) What year was the NBA formed by the merging of the Basketball Association of America and the National Basketball League?

8) The Houston Rockets franchise started in what city?

9) Against what team did Wilt Chamberlain score his 100 points in a single game?

10) What coach holds the record for most men's NCAA Division I championships?

Quiz 15 Answers

1) Russell Westbrook – Oklahoma City Thunder in 2016–17
2) Nine
3) 1954
4) 2004
5) Houston
6) Three – 1967, 1968, 1969
7) 1949
8) San Diego from 1967–1971
9) New York Knicks
10) John Wooden – 10 for UCLA

Quiz 16

1) How many feet long is a regulation NBA basketball court?
2) Who holds the NBA career record for most seasons leading the league in assists?
3) What year did the NBA and ABA merge?
4) What early NBA legend served as the first commissioner of the competing ABA league that was formed in 1967?
5) Who was the first NBA player ever to lead the league in rebounds and assists in the same season?
6) Who was the first NBA player with more than 300 blocks in a season six times?
7) Who is the first NBA player ever to average a triple-double over a season twice?
8) What was the first team to win consecutive NBA titles?
9) What player holds the single game scoring record for the men's NCAA Division I tournament?
10) What player led the NBA in total rebounds twice in the 1980s playing for Chicago but never led a season in average rebounds per game?

Quiz 16 Answers

1) 94 feet
2) John Stockton – nine
3) 1976
4) George Mikan
5) Wilt Chamberlain – 1967-68 season
6) Mark Eaton
7) Russell Westbrook – Oklahoma City Thunder in 2016-17 and 2017-18
8) Minneapolis Lakers – 1949 and 1950
9) Austin Carr – 61 points for Notre Dame in 1970
10) Charles Oakley

Quiz 17

1) Who was the first NBA player to make more than 100 three-pointers in a season?
2) What year was the first women's NCAA Division I tournament?
3) What coach won eight straight NBA championships with the Boston Celtics?
4) What was the first NBA franchise to win five championships?
5) Which NBA player scored 1,000 points or more in a season 19 times?
6) What college did John Stockton play for?
7) What NBA player scored the most points during the 1990s?
8) In the 1963 NCAA Division I men's basketball tournament, what team set a margin of victory record by defeating their opponent 111-42 in the first round?
9) What was the first NBA franchise to win 10 championships?
10) Who is the career WNBA scoring leader?

Quiz 17 Answers

1) Danny Ainge – 148 in the 1987-88 season
2) 1982
3) Red Auerbach – 1959 to 1966

4) Los Angeles Lakers – fifth championship in 1954

5) Kareem Abdul-Jabbar

6) Gonzaga

7) Karl Malone

8) Loyola – They beat Tennessee Tech and went on to win the championship.

9) Boston Celtics – 10th championship in 1968

10) Diana Taurasi

Quiz 18

1) Who was the oldest player to lead the NBA in rebounds?

2) Who was the first NBA player to score 20,000 career points?

3) Including NCAA Divisions I, II, and III, what team holds the record for most men's national basketball championships?

4) Who holds the NBA record for fewest games needed to reach 20,000 points?

5) When Lebron James broke the record to become the youngest NBA player to score 10,000 points, whose record did he break?

6) What NBA Hall of Fame player was also a pitcher for the Chicago White Sox?

7) Who was the first NBA player to get a quadruple (points, rebounds, assists, steals) double in a game?

8) Who was the first player to win both the NCAA Division I championship and the NBA title?

9) Who was the first player ever to win NCAA Division I, Olympic, and NBA championships?

10) Who holds the NBA career record for most triple-doubles?

Quiz 18 Answers

1) Dennis Rodman – 36 years old

2) Bob Pettit – 1965

3) UCLA

4) Wilt Chamberlain – 499 games

5) Kobe Bryant

6) Dave DeBusschere – He played from 1962-1974 with the Detroit

Pistons and New York Knicks and pitched for the Chicago White Sox in 1962–1963.

7) Alvin Robertson – San Antonio Spurs in 1986

8) Arnie Ferrin – 1944 NCAA champion with Utah and 1950 NBA champion with the Minneapolis Lakers

9) Clyde Lovellette – 1952 NCCAA champion with Kansas, 1952 Olympic champion, first NBA championship in 1954 with the Minneapolis Lakers

10) Oscar Robertson – 181

Quiz 19

1) Who was the first WNBA MVP?

2) Who holds the NBA career record for highest blocks per game average?

3) What WNBA team won four consecutive championships from 1997–2000?

4) What is the name of the trophy awarded annually to the NBA champion team?

5) What NBA team had the most regular season wins from 1970–1979?

6) Who is the youngest NBA player to start a game?

7) What NBA team had the most regular season wins from 1980–1989?

8) What college has won the second most NCAA Division I women's titles?

9) Who is the oldest NBA player to score 60 points in a game?

10) Who was the first player to win consecutive NBA MVP awards?

Quiz 19 Answers

1) Cynthia Cooper – 1997

2) Mark Eaton – 3.5 blocks per game

3) Houston Comets

4) Larry O'Brien Championship Trophy

5) Milwaukee Bucks (492–328)

6) Kobe Bryant – 18 years and 158 days

7) Boston Celtics (592–228)

8) Tennessee
9) Kobe Bryant - 37
10) Bill Russell in 1960-61 and 1961-62

Quiz 20

1) Who holds the NBA career record for most seasons leading the league in rebounds?
2) Who was the first WNBA player with 5,000 career points?
3) Who is the oldest NBA player to score 70 points in a game?
4) Who holds the NBA career record for most consecutive seasons leading the league in steals?
5) Who is the oldest NBA player to score 60 points in a game?
6) What NBA player scored the most points during the 2000s?
7) Shaquille O'Neal played for what college?
8) Who won three consecutive NBA MVP awards from 1984-1986?
9) What pick was Michael Jordan in the 1984 NBA draft?
10) In NCAA tournament play, what USC player was the first woman to win consecutive Final Four MVP awards?

Quiz 20 Answers

1) Wilt Chamberlain - 11
2) Lisa Leslie - 2006
3) David Robinson - 28
4) Chris Paul - six
5) Kobe Bryant - 37
6) Kobe Bryant
7) LSU
8) Larry Bird
9) Third
10) Cheryl Miller - 1983, 1984

Quiz 21

1) Who was the first NBA player to have two quadruple doubles in their career?

2) What is the minimum number of players an NBA team must have dressed in uniform and on the bench for a game?

3) Who holds the NBA career record for most consecutive seasons leading the league in assists?

4) Which team won the first college National Invitational Tournament (NIT) in 1938?

5) Who was the first center to lead the NBA in assists for a season?

6) What was the first season the NBA started counting blocks as a statistic?

7) Who are the only two NBA players who won MVP awards in their rookie season?

8) Who is the youngest NBA player to debut as a starter?

9) What is the only year in men's or women's NCAA Division I that two undefeated teams met for the national championship?

10) Who holds the NBA career record for most assists?

Quiz 21 Answers

1) Hakeem Olajuwon - Both occurred in 1990.

2) Eight

3) John Stockton - nine

4) Temple

5) Wilt Chamberlain

6) 1973-74

7) Wilt Chamberlain in 1959-60 and Wes Unseld in 1968-69

8) Lebron James - 18 years and 303 days

9) 2014 women's tournament - Connecticut beat Notre Dame 79-58

10) John Stockton - 15,806

Quiz 22

1) What player appears as the silhouette on the NBA's official logo?

2) Who holds the NBA career record for highest points per game?

3) Who is the only player to win the WNBA Championship MVP four consecutive years?

4) Who holds the NBA career record for most minutes played per game?

5) During the 1981–82 season which NBA team scored at least 100 points in every game?

6) Who was the first WNBA player with 3,000 career rebounds?

7) What year did Wilt Chamberlain score his 100 points in one game?

8) What is the NBA record for most field goals attempted by one player in a game?

9) Who was the oldest NBA player to have a triple-double?

10) What team won the first championship after the league changed its name to the NBA?

Quiz 22 Answers

1) Jerry West
2) Michael Jordan – 30.1 ppg
3) Cynthia Cooper – 1997 to 2000
4) Wilt Chamberlain – 45.8 minutes
5) Denver Nuggets
6) Lisa Leslie – 2008
7) 1962
8) 63 – Wilt Chamberlain
9) Karl Malone – 40
10) Minneapolis Lakers in 1949–50

Football

Quiz 1

1) Who was the first Heisman Trophy winner to play on a losing team the year they won?
2) Which 1970s NFL team set a record losing 26 consecutive games?
3) Who was the first NFL quarterback with 70,000 career passing yards?
4) Who was the first quarterback to lead his team to four Super Bowl titles?
5) What NCAA Division I school won the most games from 1980–1989?
6) What was the first year that 10 or more NFL players rushed for 1,000 yards in a season?
7) Who was the first NFL quarterback to start more than 200 consecutive games?
8) Who was the first NCAA Division I player to rush for 2,000 yards in a season?
9) What NFL quarterback appeared in 10 straight league championship games?
10) Who were the second pair of NFL teammates to each rush for 1,000 yards in the same season?

Quiz 1 Answers

1) Paul Hornung – Notre Dame was 2-8 in 1956 when Hornung won.
2) Tampa Bay Buccaneers – 1976 to 1977
3) Brett Favre – 2010 Minnesota Vikings
4) Terry Bradshaw – 1975, 1976, 1979,1980
5) Nebraska (103–20–0)
6) 1972
7) Brett Favre
8) Marcus Allen – 1981 USC Trojans
9) Otto Graham – 1946 to 1955 Cleveland Browns
10) Franco Harris and Rocky Bleier – 1976 Pittsburgh Steelers

Quiz 2

1) Who was the first president of the NFL?
2) What was the original name for the NFL?
3) Who is the only person to win the Heisman Trophy twice?
4) What year was the NFL formed?
5) Who retired after the 2002 NFL season and was the second player ever to play 20 seasons with one team?
6) Who was the first receiver to catch 20 touchdowns in a season?
7) What member of the Pro Football Hall of Fame became an Associate Justice of the Minnesota Supreme Court?
8) Who was the first NFL player with 100 career receiving touchdowns?
9) Who has the NFL career record for most fumbles?
10) Who was the first NFL quarterback to pass for 30 touchdowns in a season?

Quiz 2 Answers

1) Jim Thorpe
2) American Professional Football Association (APFA)
3) Archie Griffin – Ohio State in 1974 and 1975
4) 1920
5) Darrell Green – Washington Redskins from 1983-2002
6) Jerry Rice – 1987 San Francisco 49ers
7) Alan Page
8) Steve Largent – 1989 Seattle Seahawks
9) Brett Favre – 166
10) Johnny Unitas – 32 for 1959 Baltimore Colts

Quiz 3

1) What was the first college team to hold the AP number one ranking wire to wire from preseason through the bowl games?
2) What year was the first *Monday Night Football* game?
3) Who was the first NFL quarterback to throw 3,000 completions?
4) Who had the most NFL passing yards in the 1980s?

5) Who was the first player from a losing team to be named Super Bowl MVP?

6) What NCAA Division I school won the most games from 1990–1999?

7) Who broke O.J. Simpson's single season rushing record?

8) Who was the first NFL player to rush for 2,000 yards in a season?

9) What NFL team has the record for most consecutive years under .500?

10) Who was the first NFL player who wasn't a kicker to score 1,000 career points?

Quiz 3 Answers

1) Florida State – 1999

2) 1970

3) Fran Tarkenton – 1976 Minnesota Vikings

4) Joe Montana – 30,958

5) Chuck Howley – 1971 in the Dallas Cowboys loss to the Baltimore Colts

6) Florida State (109-13-1)

7) Eric Dickerson – 1984 Los Angeles Rams

8) O.J. Simpson – 1973 Buffalo Bills

9) Tampa Bay Buccaneers – 14 years from 1983–1996

10) Jerry Rice

Quiz 4

1) What NFL team had the most Super Bowl victories in the 1990s?

2) Who was the first NFL player to intercept 80 passes in their career?

3) What future NBA Hall of Fame player was selected in the seventh round of the 1962 NFL draft and was cut after one exhibition game?

4) What year did the NFL sign its first television contract for an entire season with a major network?

5) In Super Bowl XXII, who set a record for most rushing yards in a Super Bowl game?

6) The coldest NFL game in history was played where?

7) What was the first NFL team to win at least 15 games in the regular

season and not win the Super Bowl?

8) What NCAA Division I school won the most games from 1950-1959?

9) What NFL team had the most Super Bowl victories in the 1970s?

10) What is the name of the rival professional football league that merged with the NFL in 1949?

Quiz 4 Answers

1) Dallas Cowboys - three

2) Paul Krause - Washington Redskins and Minnesota Vikings from 1964-1979

3) John Havlicek - Boston Celtics 1962-1978

4) 1962

5) Timmy Smith - 204 yards for Washington Redskins

6) Green Bay – It was 13 below at kickoff for the 1967 NFL championship between the Green Bay Packers and the Dallas Cowboys.

7) New England Patriots - 2007

8) Oklahoma (93-10-2)

9) Pittsburgh Steelers - four

10) All-America Football Conference (AAFC)

Quiz 5

1) Who had the most NFL receiving yards in the 2000s?

2) Who was the first NFL head coach to take his teams to six Super Bowls?

3) What year did the first NFL indoor game take place?

4) In 1945, what Green Bay Packer became the first NFL player to score 100 career touchdowns?

5) Who held the NFL career rushing yards record before Emmitt Smith broke it?

6) Steve Largent scored 101 career touchdowns with the Seattle Seahawks; he went on to serve in the U.S. House of Representatives for what state?

7) What was the first team to appear in three consecutive Super Bowls?

8) Who had the most NFL passing yards in the 1960s?

9) Who was the first NFL player to play for the same team for 20 seasons?

10) Who was the first player selected in the first NFL draft?

Quiz 5 Answers

1) Terry Holt – 12,954

2) Don Shula

3) 1932 – With 30 below temperatures in Chicago, the Bears played a game indoors against the Portsmouth Spartans in the Chicago Stadium which was used mainly for horse shows; they played on a modified 80-yard field.

4) Don Hutson

5) Walter Payton

6) Oklahoma

7) Miami Dolphins – 1972, 1973, 1974

8) Johnny Unitas – 26,548

9) Jackie Slater – 1976-1995 with Los Angeles and St. Louis Rams

10) Jay Berwanger – He was from the University of Chicago and never ended up playing in the NFL.

Quiz 6

1) Who was the first NFL quarterback to have 40 interceptions in a season?

2) Who was the first NFL player to rush for 1,000 yards in a season?

3) What professional team had a perfect regular season and won the championship but isn't recognized as having done it because it was in a rival league that merged with the NFL in 1949?

4) Who was the first NFL rusher to run for 25 touchdowns in a season?

5) Who had the most NFL rushing yards in the 1960s?

6) What year was the first televised college game?

7) What running back was the first to throw for over 750 career yards?

8) Who was the first NFL receiver with 100 catches in a season?

9) Who was the first NFL running back with 100 catches in a season?

10) What NFL team had the most regular season wins in the 2000s?

Quiz 6 Answers

1) George Blanda – 1962 Houston Oilers
2) Beattie Feathers – 1934 Chicago Bears
3) 1948 Cleveland Browns – part of AAFC
4) Emmitt Smith – 1995 Dallas Cowboys
5) Jim Brown – 8,514
6) 1939
7) Frank Gifford – New York Giants 1952-1964
8) Lionel Taylor – 1961 Denver Broncos
9) Larry Centers – 101 catches with 1995 Arizona Cardinals
10) Indianapolis Colts (115-45)

Quiz 7

1) Who did Miami defeat in the Super Bowl to retain their perfect undefeated season?
2) In 2007, Tom Brady threw a record 50 touchdowns in a season; whose record did he break?
3) In 1966, what NFL team was the first to score 70 points in a regular season game?
4) What college did Walter Payton play for?
5) Who is the second NFL player ever to have 1,000 yards rushing and 1,000 yards receiving in a season?
6) What year was the first nationally televised college game?
7) What NFL quarterback set a single game record with 554 yards passing during the 1951 season?
8) Who was the first NFL quarterback with 6,000 career completions?
9) What NFL team has the record for the longest consecutive playoff game winning streak?
10) Who was the first coach to win more than one Super Bowl?

Quiz 7 Answers

1) Washington Redskins
2) Payton Manning – 49 for 2004 Baltimore Colts

3) Washington Redskins – in a 72–41 win over the New York Giants

4) Jackson State

5) Marshall Faulk – 1999 St. Louis Rams

6) 1952 – Stanford against Illinois in the Rose Bowl

7) Norm Van Brocklin – Los Angeles Rams

8) Brett Favre – 2009 Minnesota Vikings

9) New England Patriots – 10 games from 2002–2006

10) Vince Lombardi – Green Bay Packers in 1967 and 1968

Quiz 8

1) What was the first team to win five Super Bowls without losing one?

2) What Super Bowl winning NFL head coach also won a NASCAR Cup series championship as an owner?

3) What year was the first NFL Championship game?

4) What Pro Football Hall of Fame player once led the league in passing, interceptions, and punting in the same season?

5) What are the only three teams to lose their first four Super Bowls?

6) What NFL team had undefeated regular seasons in 1934 and 1942 but lost the NFL championship both years?

7) How did the Green Bay Packers get their name?

8) What NFL team had the most regular season wins in the 1990s?

9) Instead of the Super Bowl, what is the Canadian Football League's championship called?

10) While in college, Jim Brown was an All-American in what other sport besides football?

Quiz 8 Answers

1) San Francisco 49ers

2) Joe Gibbs – 2000 NASCAR Cup

3) 1933 – Prior to this, the champion was decided based on who had the best record.

4) Sammy Baugh – 1943 Washington Redskins

5) Minnesota Vikings, Denver Broncos, Buffalo Bills

6) Chicago Bears

7) The team founder Curly Lambeau asked his employer, The Indian Packing Company, for equipment and his employer agreed to sponsor the team if he named them the Packers.

8) San Francisco 49ers (113-47)

9) Grey Cup

10) Lacrosse - Syracuse University

Quiz 9

1) What NCAA Division I school won the most games from 1920-1929?

2) Who was the first NFL running back with 20 rushing touchdowns in a season?

3) What two teams played in the first college game?

4) In 2007, who set a record for most rushing yards in an NFL game?

5) What college team has the record for most consecutive bowl game wins?

6) Who was the first player with five Super Bowl titles?

7) What NCAA Division I school won the most games from 1960-1969?

8) Who was the first NFL head coach to lose two Super Bowls?

9) Who was the first person inducted into the Pro Football and Major League Baseball Hall of Fame?

10) Who was the first non-college player ever selected in the first round of the NFL draft?

Quiz 9 Answers

1) USC (87-13-2)

2) John Riggins - 24 for 1983 Washington Redskins

3) Rutgers and Princeton - In 1869, Rutgers beat Princeton 6-4 in a game that had 25 players on each side and one-point touchdowns; the first team to reach six points was declared the winner.

4) Adrian Peterson - 296 yards for Minnesota Vikings

5) Florida State – 11 consecutive wins from 1985-1995

6) Charles Haley - two with San Francisco 49ers and three with Dallas Cowboys

7) Alabama (90-16-4)

8) Don Shula – 1969, 1972

9) Cal Hubbard – He was an offensive lineman for New York and Green Bay in the 1920s and 1930s and was on four championship teams; he was also an MLB umpire.

10) Eric Swann – He was playing semi-professional football and was drafted by the Arizona Cardinals in 1991.

Quiz 10

1) What NCAA Division I school won the most games from 2000–2009?

2) What school won or shared the most Big 10 titles in the 20th century?

3) What NFL team had the most regular season wins in the 1970s?

4) What team won the first NFL Championship game?

5) What NFL team had the most Super Bowl victories in the 2000s?

6) Who was the first NFL coach to win 300 games?

7) Who was the first Heisman Trophy winner who did not play an offensive position?

8) What school won its first Big 10 title in 59 years in 1995?

9) What is the oldest college bowl game?

10) Who is the only person to have both a reception and an interception in the Super Bowl?

Quiz 10 Answers

1) Boise State (112–17–0)

2) Michigan – 38

3) Dallas Cowboys (105–39)

4) Chicago Bears – They defeated the New York Giants 23–21 in 1933.

5) New England Patriots – three

6) George Halas – Chicago Bears

7) Charles Woodson – 1997 Michigan

8) Northwestern

9) Rose Bowl – 1902

10) Deion Sanders – interception in Super Bowl XXIX and a reception in Super Bowl XXX

Quiz 11

1) Who was the first college player to win the Heisman, Maxwell, and O'Brien awards and become the first overall pick in the NFL draft?

2) Which U.S. President played for the University of Michigan?

3) Who had the most NFL rushing yards in the 1990s?

4) What NFL team was originally called the Senors?

5) Who was the first NFL quarterback to throw for 4,000 yards in a season?

6) Who was the first NFL running back to carry the ball 4,000 times in their career?

7) Who was the first NFL quarterback to have 10 games with 300 yards passing in a season?

8) What college team has the record for consecutive bowl game appearances?

9) Who was the first NFL player with 160 career fumbles?

10) In a 14-game season, how many times did a pair of teammates each rush for 1,000 yards in the same season?

Quiz 11 Answers

1) Vinny Testaverde - 1986 University of Miami

2) Gerald Ford

3) Emmitt Smith - 13,963

4) Oakland Raiders – The original name was winner of a name the team contest; it was changed to Raiders, the third-place name, after nine days.

5) Joe Namath - 1967 Jets

6) Emmitt Smith

7) Rich Gannon - 2002 Oakland Raiders

8) Florida State

9) Warren Moon - 1984 to 2000

10) Two - 1972 Miami Dolphins (Mercury Morris and Larry Csonka) and 1976 Pittsburgh Steelers (Franco Harris and Rocky Bleier)

Quiz 12

1) What year was the Canadian Football League founded?

2) Who held the NFL career rushing yards record before Walter Payton broke it?

3) What year was the first Army vs. Navy game?

4) Who is the oldest player ever in an NFL game?

5) What NFL team has the record for longest consecutive game winning streak including playoff games?

6) Why is the NFL Baltimore team named the ravens?

7) What NFL team has the record for the longest regular season consecutive game winning streak?

8) What NCAA Division I school won the most games from 1940–1949?

9) What was the margin of victory in the most lopsided NFL championship game ever?

10) Who was the first African American Heisman Trophy winner?

Quiz 12 Answers

1) 1958

2) Jim Brown

3) 1890

4) George Blanda – 48 years old

5) New England Patriots - 21 games in 2003-2004

6) Edgar Allen Poe who wrote *The Raven* was from Baltimore.

7) Indianapolis Colts - 23 games in 2008-2009

8) Notre Dame (82-9-6)

9) 73 points - In 1940, the Chicago Bears beat the Washington Redskins 73-0 in the NFL Championship.

10) Ernie Davis - 1961 Syracuse University

Quiz 13

1) Who was named the MVP of the first Super Bowl in 1967?

2) Who was the first NFL rusher with 5,000 career yards?

3) What NFL team has the record for longest consecutive regular season home game winning streak?

4) What NFL team was the first to win three consecutive league championships?

5) Who was the first NFL running back to carry the ball 400 times in a season?

6) Who was the first Heisman Trophy winner from a military academy?

7) What was the first NFL team to score 30 rushing touchdowns in a season?

8) What was the first AFL team to win the Super Bowl?

9) What two college teams play for the Floyd of Rosedale trophy?

10) What NFL team had the most regular season wins in the 1980s?

Quiz 13 Answers

1) Bart Starr – Green Bay Packers

2) Steve Van Buren – Philadelphia Eagles from 1944-1951

3) Miami Dolphins – 27 games from 1971-1974

4) Green Bay Packers – 1929 to 1931

5) James Wilder – 1984 Tampa Bay Buccaneers

6) Doc Blanchard – 1945 Army

7) Green Bay Packers – 1962

8) New York Jets – 1969

9) Minnesota and Iowa – It is a bronze statue of a pig.

10) San Francisco 49ers (104-47-1)

Quiz 14

1) Who was the first NFL player to score 2,000 points?

2) What year was the first college game with a halftime show featuring a marching band?

3) What is the name of the one of the oldest trophies in college football contested between Minnesota and Michigan?

4) Who set what were then NCAA records for most career yards and most yards rushing in a season in 1976?

5) What NFL team has the record for most consecutive years out of the playoffs?

6) Who left college in 1999 as the NCAA Division I career rushing yards leader?

7) Who had the most NFL receiving yards in the 1990s?

8) What is the largest margin of victory in a college game?

9) What is the first Super Bowl team to be shut out in the second half and still win?

10) Who had the most NFL receiving yards in the 1980s?

Quiz 14 Answers

1) George Blanda

2) 1907 - Chicago vs. Illinois

3) Little Brown Jug - 1892

4) Tony Dorsett - University of Pittsburgh

5) New Orleans Saints - 20 years from 1967-1986

6) Ron Dayne - Wisconsin

7) Jerry Rice - 12,078

8) 222 points - Georgia Tech beat Cumberland College 222-0 in 1916.

9) Miami Dolphins – 1973 Super Bowl against the Washington Redskins

10) James Lofton - 9,645

Quiz 15

1) Who had the most NFL rushing yards in the 1970s?

2) What was the first undefeated team to win the Super Bowl?

3) What award is certified by the NCAA as the oldest series rivalry trophy and is presented to the winner of the Arizona and Arizona State game?

4) During the 1990s, what player set a record for career sacks?

5) Who had the most NFL passing yards in the 1970s?

6) What coach leads the NFL in career wins?

7) What year was instant replay first used in the NFL

8) Who was the first NFL quarterback to defeat 32 franchises over their career?

9) Who held the NFL career rushing yards record before Jim Brown broke it?

10) What was the Heisman Trophy originally called?

Quiz 15 Answers

1) O.J. Simpson – 10,539
2) Miami Dolphins – Super Bowl VII in 1973
3) Territorial Cup – first awarded in 1899
4) Reggie White
5) Fran Tarkenton – 23,863
6) Don Shula – 347 with Baltimore Colts and Miami Dolphins
7) 1986
8) Brett Favre – 2009
9) Joe Perry – San Francisco 49ers and Baltimore Colts from 1948–1963
10) Downtown Athletic Club Award – It was renamed in 1936 after John Heisman who was the club's first athletic director.

Quiz 16

1) Who was the first soccer style kicker in the NFL?
2) Who holds the NFL career record for most extra points made?
3) Who was the first sophomore to win the Heisman Trophy?
4) Who had the most NFL rushing yards in the 1980s?
5) What was the first NFL team to make eight Super Bowl appearances?
6) Who was the first coach with four Super Bowl wins?
7) Who was the first NFL quarterback to throw for 5,000 yards in a season?
8) Who was the first freshman to win the Heisman Trophy?
9) What team won the first college BCS Championship?
10) Who was the first player with 15,000 receiving yards in their NFL career?

Quiz 16 Answers

1) Pete Gogolak – 1964 Buffalo Bills
2) George Blanda – 943 from 1949–1975
3) Tim Tebow – 2007
4) Eric Dickerson – 11,226

5) Dallas Cowboys

6) Chuck Noll – Pittsburgh Steelers – 1975, 1976, 1979,1980

7) Dan Marino – 1984 Miami Dolphins

8) Johnny Manziel – 2012

9) University of Tennessee – 1998

10) Jerry Rice – 1995 San Francisco 49ers

Quiz 17

1) Who was the NFL number one draft pick in 1961 and was Rookie of the Year and went on to win Super Bowls as both a player and a coach?

2) What is the NFL record for most interceptions thrown by one quarterback in a single game?

3) What year was the first NFL game televised?

4) Who was the first NFL player to score 20 touchdowns in a season?

5) What year did the NFL name the Super Bowl trophy after Vince Lombardi?

6) What year was the first NFL night game?

7) Who was the first NFL player to score 200 career touchdowns?

8) What is the NFL record for most consecutive road game wins?

9) What NFL franchise is the oldest?

10) Who were first pair of NFL teammates to each rush for 1,000 yards in the same season?

Quiz 17 Answers

1) Mike Ditka

2) Eight – Jim Hardy in 1950

3) 1939

4) Lenny Moore – 1964 Baltimore Colts

5) 1970

6) 1929

7) Jerry Rice

8) 18 – San Francisco 49ers from 1988–1990

9) Arizona Cardinals – 1899 in Chicago under the name of the Morgan

Athletic Club

10) Mercury Morris and Larry Csonka - 1972 Miami Dolphins

Quiz 18

1) Who was the first NFL player to rush for an average of 100 yards per game in a season?

2) Which team won the first NFL championship game to go into overtime?

3) How many feet wide is a regulation NFL football field?

4) What future nationally known politician was the first NFL quarterback to throw for 3,000 yards in a season?

5) Prior to the Super Bowl era, what team won the most NFL championships?

6) Who was the first person to lead the NFL in rushing and win the Super Bowl in the same season?

7) Who is the first player ever in both the Pro Football Hall of Fame and the Canadian Football Hall of Fame?

8) Who was the first NFL punter to average over 50 yards a punt for a season?

9) What was the first team to lose four Super Bowls?

10) What was the first team to win the Super Bowl by more than 40 points?

Quiz 18 Answers

1) Jim Brown - 1958

2) Baltimore Colts - 1958 win over the New York Giants

3) 160

4) Jack Kemp - 1960 Los Angeles Chargers

5) Green Bay Packers - nine championships over 36 years

6) Emmitt Smith - 1992 Dallas Cowboys

7) Warren Moon

8) Sammy Baugh - 51.4 yards per punt for the 1940 Washington Redskins while also playing quarterback

9) Minnesota Vikings - lost Super Bowls IV, VIII, IX, XI

10) San Francisco 49ers - They beat the Denver Broncos 55-10 in 1990.

Quiz 19

1) Who was the first person to ever play for 25 years in the NFL?
2) In 2013, who broke the NFL record for the longest field goal?
3) Who was the first player with 20,000 receiving yards in their NFL career?
4) If you include the Canadian Football League, who was the first professional quarterback with 70,000 career passing yards?
5) What year was the first college game played under lights?
6) Like many other NFL coaches, Bud Grant played professional football, but he also played what other professional sport?
7) What longtime NFL placekicker invented the Nerf football?
8) Who was the first NFL quarterback to complete 400 passes in a season?
9) What is the most common name for U.S. college football teams?
10) What college did Peyton Manning play for?

Quiz 19 Answers

1) George Blanda – He played from 1949-1975 taking off the 1959 season.
2) Matt Prater – 64 yards for Denver Broncos
3) Jerry Rice – 2001 Oakland Raiders
4) Warren Moon – 21, 228 yards in the CFL and 49,325 yards in the NFL
5) 1892
6) Basketball – Minneapolis Lakers 1949-1951
7) Fred Cox – Minnesota Vikings from 1963-1977
8) Warren Moon – 1991 Houston Oilers
9) Eagles
10) University of Tennessee

Quiz 20

1) Who were the first ever NFL quarterback and running back teammates to each rush for 1,000 yards in the same season?
2) Who was the first NFL player to have 1,000 yards rushing and 1,000

yards receiving in a season?

3) How long is the longest consecutive game winning streak in U.S. high school football history?

4) The 2007 New England Patriots had a perfect regular season but lost the Super Bowl to what team?

5) The NFL line judge position was added in 1965 largely in response to what quarterback?

6) Who set a record in 2002 for most NFL pass receptions in a season?

7) How many NFL players have at least 10,000 yards rushing and 5,000 yards receiving in their career?

8) Who had the most NFL passing yards in the 2000s?

9) What is the only team to play in the Super Bowl in the 1960s, 1970s, and 1980s?

10) What university originated the football huddle?

Quiz 20 Answers

1) Michael Vick and Warrick Dunn – 2006 Atlanta Falcons

2) Roger Craig – 1985 San Francisco 49ers

3) 151 games – De La Salle Spartans from Concord, California from 1991–2004

4) New York Giants

5) Fran Tarkenton – His scrambling style forced the need for a line judge to monitor line of scrimmage infractions.

6) Marvin Harrison – 143 for Baltimore Colts

7) Three – Marshall Faulk, Marcus Allen, Tiki Barber

8) Peyton Manning – 42,254

9) Oakland Raiders – 1968, 1977, 1981, 1984

10) Gallaudet University (school for the deaf) in 1892 – They huddled to avoid the other team seeing their sign language.

Quiz 21

1) What was the first team to appear in four consecutive Super Bowls?

2) What was the first team to lose three Super Bowls?

3) What year was the first NFL draft?

4) What is the only community owned franchise in the NFL?

5) What NCAA Division I school won the most games from 1930-1939?

6) Who is the first NFL player with seven career 2-point conversions?

7) What NFL team had the most Super Bowl victories in the 1980s?

8) In 1954, what was the first NFL team with a cheerleading squad?

9) Who was the first quarterback to win Super Bowl MVP without throwing a touchdown?

10) Who had the most NFL rushing yards in the 2000s?

Quiz 21 Answers

1) Buffalo Bills - 1991, 1992, 1993, 1994

2) Minnesota Vikings - lost Super Bowls IV, VIII, IX

3) 1936 - There were nine rounds.

4) Green Bay Packers

5) Texas Christian University (84-24-8)

6) Marshall Faulk

7) San Francisco 49ers - four

8) Baltimore Colts

9) Joe Namath - 1969

10) LaDainian Tomlinson - 12,490

Quiz 22

1) Who had the most NFL passing yards in the 1990s?

2) Who was the first college player to be a three-time unanimous, consensus All-American?

3) What NCAA Division I school won the most games from 1970-1979?

4) What was the last NFL team Franco Harris played for?

5) Who is the oldest NFL player to rush for 150 yards in a game?

6) Who was the first NFL running back to rush for 100 career touchdowns?

7) What college was the first to have seven Heisman Trophy winners?

8) Who was the first NFL quarterback to throw 200 career touchdown passes?

9) What college team has won the most Rose Bowls?

10) What 1970s NFL team was the first to rush for 3,000 yards in a

season?

11) Instant replay was first used in any sports broadcast in the Army vs. Navy game in what year?

Quiz 22 Answers

1) Dan Marino – 33,508

2) Herschel Walker – Georgia in 1980, 1981, 1982

3) Alabama (103-16-1)

4) Seattle Seahawks – 1984

5) John Riggins – 35 years old

6) Jim Brown – Cleveland Browns from 1957–1965

7) Notre Dame – Angelo Bertelli (1943), John Lujack (1947), Leon Hart (1949), John Lattner (1952), Paul Hornung (1956), John Huarte (1964), Tim Brown (1987)

8) Y.A. Tittle – 1962 New York Giants

9) USC

10) Buffalo Bills (1973) – O.J. Simpson rushed for 2,003 yards.

11) 1963

Hockey

Quiz 1

1) What year did the NHL implement the modern offside rule?
2) What was the first American team to win two Stanley Cups?
3) Who was the first defenseman after Bobby Orr to win the Hart Trophy and Norris Trophy in the same year?
4) What two teammates finished one and two in the NHL scoring race five times?
5) How many seasons did Gordie Howe play professional hockey?
6) Who was the first American NHL player with 50 goals in a season?
7) Who is the youngest player inducted into the Hockey Hall of Fame?
8) What team won four Stanley Cups in a row from 1980-1983?
9) Who was the last Conn Smythe Trophy winner in the 20th century to be on the defeated team in the Stanley Cup finals?
10) Who has the NHL record for most goals in a season by a rookie?

Quiz 1 Answers

1) 1930
2) New York Rangers – 1928, 1933
3) Chris Pronger – St. Louis Blues 1999–00
4) Phil Esposito and Bobby Orr
5) 32
6) Bobby Carpenter – Washington Capitals 1984–85
7) Bobby Orr – 31 years old
8) New York Islanders
9) Ron Hextall – 1987 Philadelphia Flyers
10) Teemu Selanne – 76 goals in 1992–93 season for Winnipeg Jets

Quiz 2

1) What NHL team had the most regular season wins from 1950–1959?
2) What NHL team set a record for most consecutive playoff

appearances with 25 seasons from 1979-2004?

3) What two NHL players are tied for most goals in a season by a European?

4) Who played the most consecutive NHL games as a goaltender?

5) What award is given annually to the leading NHL goal scorer?

6) Who is credited as the NHL goalie who developed and made the first effective use of the butterfly style of goalkeeping?

7) What NHL player was the first to have 3,000 career penalty minutes?

8) Who was the first defenseman to win the Calder Memorial Trophy as top NHL rookie?

9) Who was the first Czech player drafted number one overall in the NHL draft?

10) Who was the first woman to have her name engraved on the Stanley Cup?

Quiz 2 Answers

1) Detroit Red Wings (362-208-130)

2) St. Louis Blues

3) Teemu Selanne and Alexander Mogilny - 76 goals each in the 1992-93 season

4) Glenn Hall - 502 games from 1955-1962

5) Maurice Richard Trophy

6) Glenn Hall

7) David "Tiger" Williams - played from 1974-1988

8) Kent Douglas - Toronto Maple Leafs 1962-63

9) Roman Hamrlik - 1992 Tampa Bay Lightning

10) Marguerite Norris - In 1952, she became the first female chief executive in NHL history after inheriting the Detroit Red Wings presidency from her father James Norris Sr. on his death. In 1954, the Red Wings defeated the Montreal Canadiens making her the first woman to have her name engraved on the Stanley Cup.

Quiz 3

1) Who was the last goalie to play every game for his team in a season?

2) What NHL defenseman has the most career regular season assists?

3) When Wayne Gretzky broke the season goal scoring record in 1981–82 with 92 goals, whose record did he break?

4) What NHL team has the record for the longest consecutive playoff game losing streak?

5) How many times did Gordie Howe win the Hart Memorial Trophy as league MVP?

6) What NHL defenseman has the most career regular season goals?

7) Who was the first NHL player with 500 career goals?

8) What NHL player never missed a regular season game in his career and holds the record for most consecutive games played at 964?

9) What American citizen NHL player has the most career regular season points?

10) What American born NHL defenseman has the most career points?

Quiz 3 Answers

1) Eddie Johnston – Boston Bruins 1964–64

2) Ray Bourque – 1,169 assists

3) Phil Esposito – 76 goals

4) Chicago Blackhawks – 16 games from 1975–1979

5) Six – 1952, 1953, 1957, 1958, 1960, 1963

6) Ray Bourque – 410 goals

7) Maurice Richard – 500th in 1957

8) Doug Jarvis – played from 1975–1987

9) Brett Hull – 1,391 points

10) Phil Housley – 1,232 points

Quiz 4

1) Of the teams added in the 1967 NHL expansion, which two either no longer exist or have moved?

2) How many consecutive years did Gordie Howe finish in the top 10 in the NHL scoring race?

3) The Original Six are the six NHL teams that made up the league from 1942 until the 1967 expansion; what are the Original Six teams?

4) What NHL team won four Stanley Cups in five years from 1984–1988?

5) What is the only jersey number retired league wide by the NHL?

6) What NHL team had the most regular season wins from 1970–1979?

7) At the time he retired, how many NHL records did Wayne Gretzky hold?

8) How many seasons did Wayne Gretzky play in the WHA?

9) Who was the first NHL rookie to score 50 goals in a season?

10) What Swedish NHL player has the most career regular season goals?

Quiz 4 Answers

1) California Seals and Minnesota North Stars – The Seals became the Cleveland Barons in 1976 and merged with the Minnesota North Stars in 1978. The North Stars moved to Dallas in 1993.

2) 21 years

3) Boston Bruins, Chicago Black Hawks, Detroit Red Wings, Montreal Canadiens, New York Rangers, Toronto Maple Leafs

4) Edmonton Oilers

5) 99 – Wayne Gretzky

6) Montreal Canadiens (499-155-134)

7) 61

8) One – He entered the WHA in the 1978–79 season; the WHA merged into the NHL the following season.

9) Mike Bossy– 53 for New York Islanders in 1977–78

10) Mats Sundin – 584 goals

Quiz 5

1) Who was the first Conn Smythe Trophy winner in the 21st century to be on the defeated team in the Stanley Cup finals?

2) From 1924–2018, how many NHL Art Ross Trophy winners as the league's leading scorer have been American born?

3) What NHL defenseman has the most assists in a season?

4) What NHL team has the most regular season wins from 1990–1999?

5) Who was the first Russian player drafted number one overall in the NHL draft?

6) Who was the Detroit Red Wings coach when they won Stanley Cups in 1997, 1998, and 2002?

7) Who was the first NHL player penalized 400 minutes in one season?

8) What Russian NHL player has the most career regular season goals?

9) In feet, how wide is a regulation NHL rink?

10) Who won the inaugural 1996 World Cup of Hockey?

Quiz 5 Answers

1) Jean-Sebastien Giguere – 2003 Anaheim Mighty Ducks

2) One – Patrick Kane in 2016

3) Bobby Orr – 102 assists in 1970-71

4) Detroit Red Wings (418-264-102)

5) Ilya Kovalchuk – 2001 Atlanta Thrashers

6) Scotty Bowman

7) Dave Schultz – Philadelphia Flyers 1974-75

8) Alexander Ovechkin

9) 85 feet

10) United States

Quiz 6

1) What Czech NHL player has the most career regular season points?

2) Who was the second NHL player to score 50 goals in 50 games?

3) Who was the first non-Canadian NHL player to score 500 career goals?

4) What are the names of the six Sutter brothers who all played in the NHL?

5) What was the first American team to play in the Stanley Cup Finals?

6) What NHL player has the largest differential ever between their goals and assists in one season?

7) Who has won the most Vezina Trophies as the NHL's best goaltender?

8) What NHL team has the record for most consecutive years in the playoffs?

9) Who was the first European player drafted number one overall in the NHL draft?

10) Who was the first American player drafted number one overall in the NHL draft?

Quiz 6 Answers

1) Jaromir Jagr – 1,921 points

2) Mike Bossy – New York Islanders 1980–81

3) Jari Kurri – 500th in 1992

4) Brent, Brian, Darryl, Duane, Rich, Ron

5) Portland Rosebuds – 1916

6) Brett Hull – 86 goals and 45 assists for a differential of 41 in 1990–91 season

7) Jacques Plante – seven in the 1950s and 1960s

8) Boston Bruins – 29 years from 1968–1996

9) Mats Sundin (Sweden) – 1989 Quebec Nordiques

10) Brian Lawton – 1983 Minnesota North Stars

Quiz 7

1) Who was the first NHL goaltender to be credited with a goal?

2) Who was the first NHL player to score 50 goals in six consecutive seasons?

3) Who was the first American born player to win the Hart Memorial Trophy as league MVP?

4) What American NHL defenseman has the most career regular season assists?

5) At what age did Wayne Gretzky become a professional?

6) Who has the most Stanley Cup wins combined as player and non-player?

7) In what country was the first professional hockey league formed?

8) Who was the first player to win the Conn Smythe Trophy for Stanley Cup playoff MVP two consecutive years?

9) Which NHL team is known to their fans as the Habs?

10) What is the NHL record for career goals by a goalie?

Quiz 7 Answers

1) Billy Smith – He was playing for the New York Islanders in a 1979 game when the Colorado Rockies passed the puck back to the blueline where it went the length of the ice and into their own vacated net. Smith was the last Islander to touch the puck and was credited with the goal.

2) Guy Lafleur – Montreal Canadiens 1975–1980

3) Patrick Kane – 2016

4) Phil Housley – 894 assists

5) 17

6) Jean Beliveau – 17 with 10 as player and seven as non-player with the Montreal Canadiens

7) United States – The International Pro Hockey League based in Michigan operated for the 1910–11 season.

8) Bernie Parent – 1974 and 1975 Philadelphia Flyers

9) Montreal Canadiens – The "H" on their jersey stands for hockey from "Club de Hockey Canadien"; however, in 1924, Tex Rickard who owned Madison Square Garden told a reporter that it stood for "Habitants" from the French "Les Habitants" for the early French settlers in Canada which was shortened to Habs.

10) Two – Ron Hextall and Martin Brodeur

Quiz 8

1) In the 22 seasons between 1980–81 and 2001–02, three players won 21 of the 22 Art Ross Trophies; who were they?

2) What team has the record for the most consecutive Stanley Cup wins?

3) What NHL player has been in the most playoff games?

4) Who won the most Norris Trophies awarded to the NHL's top defensive player?

5) Which NHL team had the most regular season wins from 1960–1969?

6) In feet, how long is a regulation NHL rink?

7) What American NHL defenseman has scored the most points in a season?

8) Which two NHL teams tied for the most regular season wins from 1980–1989?

9) When the New York Rangers won the Stanley Cup in 1994, how long had it been since their prior Stanley Cup win?

10) Which NHL team has the most regular season wins from 2000–2009?

Quiz 8 Answers

1) Wayne Gretzky (10 times), Jaromir Jagr (five times), Mario Lemieux (six times)

2) Montreal Canadiens – five from 1956–1960

3) Chris Chelios – 266 games

4) Bobby Orr – eight

5) Montreal Canadiens (384-201-125)

6) 200 feet

7) Brian Leetch – 102 points in 1991–92

8) Edmonton Oilers (446-250-104) and Philadelphia Flyers (446-254-100)

9) 54 years – 1940

10) Detroit Red Wings (457-231-50)

Quiz 9

1) Who was the first NHL goaltender to score a goal by taking an intentional shot?

2) Where did ice hockey originate?

3) Who was the first player to win the Hart Trophy as the NHL's MVP by unanimous vote?

4) What American NHL defenseman has the most assists in a season?

5) What NHL player was known as "The Golden Jet"?

6) What was the first NHL American team to win five Stanley Cups?

7) What NHL team has the record for the longest consecutive game losing streak?

8) What player was the first to win one of the major NHL trophies eight consecutive years?

9) What American born NHL player has the most assists in a season?

10) What NHL player has the second most career regular season goals?

Quiz 9 Answers

1) Ron Hextall – 1987 Philadelphia Flyers

2) United Kingdom – There are references to similar games being played on ice in England, Scotland, and Ireland going back 200 years before the first documented game in Canada.

3) Wayne Gretzky – 1982

4) Brian Leetch – 80 assists in 1991-92

5) Bobby Hull

6) Detroit Red Wings – 1936, 1937, 1943, 1950, 1952

7) Washington Capitals – 20 games in 1975

8) Bobby Orr – won eight consecutive Norris Trophies from 1968-1975

9) Pat Lafontaine – 95 assists in 1992-93

10) Gordie Howe – 801 goals

Quiz 10

1) Who was the first African American NHL player?

2) What team has the record for the most consecutive Stanley Cup finals appearances?

3) What was the first U.S. hockey team to win the Stanley Cup?

4) Who is the only NHL player who won an award so often they let him keep it?

5) What NHL team has the record for most consecutive years below .500?

6) In 1976, which NHL defenseman won the Norris Trophy preventing Bobby Orr from winning his ninth consecutive award?

7) What is the record for most consecutive times a player has won the Hart Memorial Trophy as the NHL's MVP?

8) What player holds the record for most NHL career penalty minutes?

9) How tall is a regulation NHL goal from the ice to the bottom of the post?

10) How many times in NHL history has one goalie been credited with scoring a goal against an opposing goalie (not an empty net goal)?

Quiz 10 Answers

1) Willie O'Ree - 1958 Boston Bruins

2) Montreal Canadiens - 10 from 1951-1960

3) Seattle Metropolitans in 1917 - The next season the National Hockey Association was replaced by the NHL.

4) Frank Boucher - He won the Lady Byng Memorial Trophy seven times in eight years with the New York Rangers in the 1920s and 1930s.

5) Vancouver Canucks - 15 years from 1977-1991

6) Dennis Potvin

7) Eight - Wayne Gretzky from 1980-1987

8) David "Tiger" Williams - 3,971 minutes from 1974-1988

9) Four feet

10) Once - On March 21, 2013, during a game between the New Jersey Devils and Carolina Hurricanes, a delayed penalty was called against New Jersey, and Carolina goalie Dan Ellis headed for the bench for the extra attacker. After he left the crease, the Hurricanes accidentally sent the puck the length of the ice back toward their empty net; Ellis tried to race back, but he was too late. Because Devils goalie Martin Brodeur had been the last to touch the puck, he was given credit for the goal, and because Ellis was on the ice when the puck went in, the goal went on his record.

Quiz 11

1) Who was the first goalie to win two Hart Trophies?

2) Where is the Hockey Hall of Fame located?

3) Who was the first NHL player to score 50 goals in a season?

4) What American citizen NHL player has the most career regular season goals?

5) What non-Canadian NHL player has scored the most points in a season?

6) What was the first American NHL team to win three consecutive Stanley Cups?

7) What NHL team has the record for the longest consecutive game winning streak?

8) What year did the NHL allow forward passing which more than

doubled the number of goals?

9) How many goals did Wayne Gretzky score during his final season of Pee Wee hockey?

10) How many seasons did Wayne Gretzky win the Art Ross Trophy for leading the league in scoring?

Quiz 11 Answers

1) Dominik Hasek – Buffalo Sabres in 1997 and 1998

2) Toronto

3) Maurice Richard

4) Brett Hull – 741 goals

5) Jaromir Jagr – 149 points in 1995–96

6) New York Islanders – 1980 to 1982

7) Pittsburgh Penguins – 17 games in 1993

8) 1929

9) 378

10) 10

Quiz 12

1) Who was the first player to score 70 goals in an NHL season?

2) Who was the first NHL player with 100 assists in a season?

3) How many times did Wayne Gretzky score 50 goals in the first 50 games of the season?

4) Who was the first NHL player to score 100 points in six consecutive seasons?

5) Who was the first American born NHL player to reach 500 career goals?

6) What Finnish NHL player has the most career regular season goals?

7) What is the record for the most consecutive times a player has won the Art Ross Trophy as the NHL's leading scorer?

8) Who coached the Edmonton Oiler when they won four Stanley Cups from 1984–1988?

9) Who won the 2016 World Cup of Hockey?

10) What team was swept 4–0 in three consecutive Stanley Cup Finals?

Quiz 12 Answers

1) Phil Esposito - 76 in 1970-71
2) Bobby Orr - Boston Bruins 1970-71
3) Three - in 1981-82, 1983-84, and 1984-85 seasons
4) Bobby Orr - 1969 to 1975
5) Joey Mullen - 500th in 1997
6) Teemu Selanne - 684 goals
7) Seven - Wayne Gretzky from 1981-1987
8) Glen Sather
9) Canada
10) St. Louis Blues - 1968 (Montreal), 1969 (Montreal), 1970 (Boston)

Quiz 13

1) What was the last all Canadian born team to win the Stanley Cup?
2) What year was the first time an NHL team pulled their goalie to have an extra attacker?
3) What American born NHL defenseman has scored the most goals in a season?
4) What NHL goalie has the most career regular season wins?
5) What year was the five-minute sudden-death overtime implemented in the NHL for regular season games?
6) What American born NHL player has scored the most points in a season?
7) With the 1967 expansion, the NHL went from six teams to how many?
8) How many NHL players have scored 50 goals in the first 50 games of the season more than once?
9) What NHL player has the second most career regular season points?
10) What was the first American team to join the NHL?

Quiz 13 Answers

1) Philadelphia Flyers 1974-75
2) 1931 - The Boston Bruins pulled their goalie in a playoff game

against the Montreal Canadiens.

3) Kevin Hatcher – 34 goals in 1992–93

4) Martin Brodeur – 691 wins

5) 1983

6) Pat Lafontaine – 148 points in 1992–93

7) 12

8) Two – Wayne Gretzky and Brett Hull

9) Jaromir Jagr – 1,921 points

10) Boston Bruins – 1924

Quiz 14

1) What year was the first recorded indoor hockey game?

2) Who was the first NHL goalie with 500 career wins?

3) What Finnish NHL player has the most career regular season points?

4) Who was the first woman to appear in any NHL game?

5) What Czech NHL player has the most career regular season goals?

6) What Finnish NHL player has the most career regular season assists?

7) During how many decades did Gordie Howe play professional hockey?

8) What year was the Stanley Cup first awarded?

9) What is the NHL record for most goals in a single game by one player?

10) What was the first WHA team Wayne Gretzky played for?

Quiz 14 Answers

1) 1875 – Montreal

2) Patrick Roy – 2001

3) Teemu Selanne – 1,457 points

4) Manon Rheaume – She goaltended for the Tampa Bay Lightning in a pre-season game against the St. Louis Blues in September 1992.

5) Jaromir Jagr – 766 goals

6) Jari Kurri – 797 assists

7) Six – 1945 to 1998

8) 1893

9) Seven – Joe Malone for the 1920 Quebec Bulldogs

10) Indianapolis Racers – He only played eight games with the Racers before being sold to the Edmonton Oilers.

Quiz 15

1) Who was the second American player ever drafted number one overall in the NHL draft?

2) Who won the Calder Trophy for rookie of the year in Wayne Gretzky's first NHL season in 1979–80?

3) Who was the second NHL player with 500 career goals?

4) What year was the Zamboni first used in the NHL?

5) What is the NHL record for most points in a single game by one player?

6) Who was the first NHL goaltender to create and wear a practical mask?

7) How many NHL teams did Wayne Gretzky play for?

8) What NHL player has the second most career regular season assists?

9) What NHL defenseman scored the most points in a season?

10) What year did the NHL allow goalies to drop to the ice to make saves?

Quiz 15 Answers

1) Mike Modano – 1988 Minnesota North Stars

2) Ray Bourque (Boston Bruins) – Gretzky had played one WHA season making him ineligible for the award.

3) Gordie Howe – 500th in 1962

4) 1954

5) 10 – Darryl Sittler for Toronto Maple Leafs in 1976

6) Jacques Plante – 1959

7) Four – Edmonton Oilers, Los Angeles Kings, St. Louis Blues, New York Rangers

8) Ron Francis – 1,249 assists

9) Bobby Orr - 139 points (102 assists, 37 goals) for 1970-71 Boston Bruins

10) 1917 - Prior to this, goaltenders were required to remain standing.

Quiz 16

1) Who was the first non-Canadian NHL player to have 100 points in a season?

2) What two NHL players are tied for the most goals in a season by an American born player?

3) What American born NHL defenseman has the most career regular season goals?

4) What is the NHL record for most saves in a single game?

5) From 1924-2018, how many NHL Hart Memorial Trophy winners as the league's MVP have been American born?

6) What four teams joined the NHL with the merger with the WHA?

7) What NHL team has the record for most consecutive years above .500?

8) Who has won the most Lady Byng Memorial Trophies for NHL sportsmanship?

9) Who was the first Conn Smythe Trophy winner to be on the defeated team in the Stanley Cup finals?

10) Who was the first goalie to win the Hart Trophy as league MVP after Jacques Plante in 1962?

Quiz 16 Answers

1) Kent Nilsson (Sweden) - 131 points for 1980-81 Calgary Flames

2) Jimmy Carson (1987-88) and Kevin Stevens (1992-93) – 55 goals

3) Phil Housley - 338 goals

4) 92 - In a 1936 playoff game against the Montreal Maroons, Detroit Red Wings goalie Normie Smith went six overtimes and recorded a 1-0 shutout facing 92 shots in 116 minutes and 30 seconds of play also making it the longest game in NHL history.

5) One - Patrick Kane in 2016

6) Edmonton Oilers, New England Whalers, Quebec Nordiques, Winnipeg Jets

7) Montreal Canadiens - 32 years from 1952-1983

8) Frank Boucher - seven with the New York Rangers in the 1920s and 1930s

9) Roger Crozier - 1966 Detroit Red Wings

10) Dominik Hasek – 1997

Quiz 17

1) Who is the first NHL player to lead three different Canadian teams in scoring?

2) Who played from 1971-1989 and retired as one of the NHL's top scorers with eight seasons with more than 100 points but never won a Stanley Cup?

3) Who broke Bobby Orr's NHL record for most goals by a defenseman in a season?

4) What college did Brett Hull play for?

5) What Swedish NHL player has the most career regular season assists?

6) Who holds the NHL record for career shorthanded goals?

7) How many NHL players have scored 50 goals in the first 50 games of the season?

8) What is the NHL record for most shorthanded goals on a single penalty?

9) Who was the third NHL player to score 500 career goals?

10) What is the fastest time to record a hat-trick in an NHL game?

Quiz 17 Answers

1) Vincent Damphousse - Montreal, Toronto, Edmonton

2) Marcel Dionne

3) Paul Coffey - 48 goals with 1985-86 Edmonton Oilers

4) University of Minnesota, Duluth

5) Nicklas Lidstrom - 878 assists

6) Wayne Gretzky - 73

7) Five - Maurice Richard, Mike Bossy, Wayne Gretzky, Mario Lemieux, Brett Hull

8) Three - Boston Bruins in 2010

9) Bobby Hull - 500th in 1970

10) 21 seconds – Billy Mosienko in 1952

Quiz 18

1) Why was the 1919 Stanley Cup final canceled?

2) Who was the first NHL player to score 100 points in a season?

3) What was the first American NHL team to win four consecutive Stanley Cups?

4) At what age did Gordie Howe play his last professional hockey game?

5) Excluding goalies, what is the most consecutive games an NHL player has gone without scoring a goal?

6) What was the first team to win the Stanley Cup?

7) What is the NHL record for most points scored by a goalie in a game?

8) What NHL goalie played his entire career without ever recording a shutout and holds the record for most consecutive games without a shutout?

9) What NHL defenseman has the most career regular season points?

10) What is the NHL record for most shorthanded goals in a game by a single player?

Quiz 18 Answers

1) Spanish flu epidemic – It had killed Montreal Canadiens defenseman Joe Hall; the league didn't want any other people to get sick, so they canceled the Stanley cup final.

2) Phil Esposito – 126 points (49 goals, 77 assists) for 1968–69 Boston Bruins

3) New York Islanders – 1980 to 1983

4) 52

5) 255 games – defenseman Ken Daneyko for New Jersey Devils

6) Montreal Hockey Club

7) Three – Goalie Jeff Reese had three assists in a 13–1 Calgary Flames victory over the San Jose Sharks in 1993.

8) Eldon "Pokey" Reddick – played from 1986–1994

9) Ray Bourque – 1,579 points

10) Three – Theoren Fleury in 1991 in an 8–4 victory for Calgary over

St. Louis

Quiz 19

1) What Swedish NHL player has the most career regular season points?

2) In terms of number of games played, who was the second fastest NHL player to 500 career goals?

3) What year did the NHL expand from six teams to twelve?

4) Who was the first American born NHL player to win the Art Ross Trophy as the league's leading scorer?

5) Who was the first NHL player to use a slapshot?

6) Who was the first American citizen NHL player to score 500 career goals?

7) What year was the first NCAA men's hockey tournament?

8) What NHL goalie has the most career playoff wins?

9) Who holds the NHL season record for most penalty minutes by a goalie?

10) What was the first American NHL team to win two consecutive Stanley Cups?

Quiz 19 Answers

1) Mats Sundin – 1,349 points

2) Mario Lemieux – 605 games

3) 1967

4) Patrick Kane – 2016

5) Bernie Geoffrion – 1951

6) Brett Hull – 500th in 1996

7) 1948

8) Patrick Roy – 151 wins

9) Ron Hextall – 113 minutes in 1988–89 season

10) Detroit Red Wings – 1936, 1937

Quiz 20

1) What year did the World Hockey Association fold and four of its teams join the NHL?

2) How many seasons did Wayne Gretzky score 200 points or more?

3) What NHL team has the record for the longest consecutive playoff game winning streak?

4) How wide is a regulation NHL goal between the posts?

5) In the 1981–82 season, Wayne Gretzky set an NHL record for scoring 50 goals in the fewest number of games starting the season; how many games?

6) Wayne Gretzky had a brother who played part of a season in the NHL, what was his name?

7) Who was the first American born NHL player to score 100 points in a season?

8) What player has won the most Stanley Cups?

9) What was the first American NHL team that exists today to win the Stanley Cup?

10) What NHL player recorded the most penalty minutes ever in a season?

Quiz 20 Answers

1) 1979

2) Four

3) Pittsburgh Penguins – 14 games from 1992–1993

4) Six feet

5) 39

6) Brent – Tampa Bay Lightning 1993–94

7) Neal Broten – 105 points for 1985–86 Minnesota North Stars

8) Henri Richard – 11 with the Montreal Canadiens

9) New York Rangers – 1928

10) Dave Schultz – 472 minutes for 1974–75 Philadelphia Flyers

Olympics

Quiz 1

1) Who were the first two American cross-country skiers to ever win Olympic gold medals?

2) With four miles to go in the 2004 Athens men's marathon, something unusual happened to Vanderlei de Lima of Brazil who was leading by almost 30 seconds; what happened?

3) Who was the first American to win the Olympic marathon gold medal?

4) How old was the oldest Summer Olympic medalist?

5) What is the record for the most Olympic games anyone has ever competed in?

6) Who was the first African American to win an Olympic gold medal?

7) What was the last country to host both the summer and the winter Olympic games in the same year?

8) Who won the men's singles gold medal when tennis returned to the Olympics in 1988?

9) What were the only Olympics where distances were measured in yards?

10) Between winter and summer games, how many times did France host the Olympics in the 20th century?

Quiz 1 Answers

1) Jessie Diggins and Kikkan Randall – golds in women's team sprint at 2018 Pyeongchang Olympics

2) He was tackled to the ground by a spectator. Officials arrived and pulled the spectator off, and de Lima continued the race, but he was subsequently caught and passed and ended up winning the bronze medal. He filed a protest which was not upheld.

3) Frank Shorter – 1972 Munich

4) 72 years old - shooting in 1920

5) 10 - A Canadian equestrian rider competed in every Olympics from 1972 to 2012 except the boycotted 1980 games; he has one silver medal in 2008.

6) John Taylor – track and field medley relay at 1908 London games

7) Germany – 1936

8) Miloslav Mecir – Czechoslovakia

9) St. Louis – 1904

10) Five – Summer games in Paris (1900, 1924), winter games in Chamonix (1924), Grenoble (1968), Albertville (1992)

Quiz 2

1) What were the first two women's sports included in the modern Olympics?

2) From 1928 to 1968, every men's field hockey gold was won by either India or Pakistan; what country broke the dominance and won gold in 1972?

3) What famous U.S. general placed fifth in the pentathlon at the 1912 Olympics?

4) What will be the first city to host both the summer and winter Olympics?

5) What is the record for most gold medals won by an individual in a single Olympics?

6) Who was the first American woman to win four gold medals in a single Olympics?

7) What Olympics introduced beach volleyball?

8) At which games were women first allowed to compete in track and field?

9) To allow visitors to travel safely to Olympia, what was put in place before and during each of the ancient Olympic games?

10) Who was the first African American woman to win an Olympic gold medal?

Quiz 2 Answers

1) Tennis and golf

2) West Germany

3) George S. Patton

4) Beijing – 2008 summer and 2022 winter

5) Eight – Michael Phelps in swimming in 2008 Beijing Olympics

6) Amy Van Dyken – swimming at 1996 Atlanta Olympics

7) 1996 Atlanta

8) 1928 Amsterdam

9) A truce or Ekecheiria – Wars were suspended; legal disputes were put on hold, and no death penalties were carried out during this time.

10) Alice Coachman – high jump at 1948 London Olympics

Quiz 3

1) How many events were there in the first ancient Olympics?

2) What year did the Jamaican bobsled team debut at the Winter Olympics?

3) What year was the Olympic flag first flown?

4) What country did the U.S. defeat in the men's hockey gold medal game in Lake Placid in 1980?

5) What were the first Olympics held in the southern hemisphere?

6) What male athlete has the most career gymnastics medals?

7) Who won the ladies' singles figure skating event in three straight Olympics?

8) Who won the only gold medal for the U.S. at the 1968 winter Olympics?

9) What former Olympian lit the flame at the 1996 Atlanta Olympic games?

10) The Olympic triathlon consists of a 40 km bike ride and a 10 km run plus how long of a swim?

Quiz 3 Answers

1) One – a foot race

2) 1988 Calgary

3) 1920

4) Finland – They defeated the Soviet Union 4-3 in the semi-final "Miracle on Ice" game.

5) Melbourne, Australia – 1956

6) Nikolai Andrianov (Soviet Union) – 15 medals from 1972-1980

7) Sonja Henie – 1928, 1932, 1936

8) Peggy Fleming – figure skating

9) Muhammad Ali

10) 1.5 km

Quiz 4

1) In what three Olympic games were there boycotts by various Olympic teams?

2) What were the first Olympics where a swimming pool was used for swimming events?

3) Who set a long jump world record at the 1968 Mexico City Olympics that would stand for 23 years?

4) St. Louis hosted the third modern Olympics in 1904, but the Olympics were not originally scheduled to be held there; what city was the original choice?

5) What three nations have taken part in every Winter and Summer Games?

6) How old was the youngest Olympic medalist ever in an individual event?

7) A Danish journalist covering the 1900 Paris Olympics won a gold medal; how?

8) What woman won running gold medals in the 100 meters, 200 meters, and 4 x 100 meters relay in the 1988 Seoul games?

9) The 1988 Nagano Winter Olympics saw the debut of women's ice hockey, snowboarding, and what sport?

10) Who was the first person to win a gold medal in three different Olympics?

Quiz 4 Answers

1) 1976 Montreal, 1980 Moscow, 1984 Los Angeles

2) 1908 London

3) Bob Beamon (U.S.) – His jump of 29 feet 2 1/2 inches was more than 21 inches better than the prior world record.

4) Chicago – The games were relocated to St. Louis since it was hosting the World's Fair at the time.

5) France, Switzerland, Great Britain

6) 12 years old – 200 meters women's breaststroke swimming in 1936

7) He was recruited to replace an ill team member on the combined Sweden/Denmark tug of war team, and they went on to win gold.

8) Florence Griffith Joyner – U.S.

9) Curling

10) Sonja Henie – figure skating in 1928, 1932, 1936

Quiz 5

1) Cricket was only an Olympic sport once in 1900; what country won the gold?

2) What country won the most gold medals at the 2008 Beijing Summer Olympics?

3) What country won the first gold medal awarded in the modern Olympics?

4) What was the first Olympics to have an official mascot?

5) What was the first Olympics with an athlete's village?

6) How many total Olympic medals did Mark Spitz win?

7) What year did table tennis debut as a medal sport?

8) Who had the first hole-in-one during an Olympic golf tournament?

9) Who is the youngest male track and field gold medalist ever?

10) Who is the only person to win gold medals in both indoor and beach volleyball?

Quiz 5 Answers

1) Great Britain

2) China – 48 gold medals

3) United States – triple jump in 1896

4) 1968 Grenoble Winter Olympics – The mascot was Schuss, a skier.

5) 1924 Paris

6) 11 – He won seven gold medals in Munich in 1972 and two gold team medals and an individual silver and bronze in Mexico City in 1968.

7) 1988 Seoul

8) Justin Rose (Great Britain) – 2016 Rio de Janeiro

9) Bob Mathias (U.S.) – He was 17 years old when he won the 1948 decathlon.

10) Karch Kiraly (U.S.) – 1984 and 1988 indoor volleyball gold medals and 1996 beach volleyball gold

Quiz 6

1) Who was the first person to repeat as decathlon gold medalist?

2) Who duplicated Jesse Owens' feat by winning four track and field gold medals in the 100 meters, 200 meters, long jump, and 4 x 100 meters relay in 1984?

3) How old was figure skater Sonja Henie when she first participated in the Olympics in 1924?

4) Who was the first gymnast to score a perfect 10 in the Olympics?

5) In the 1924 Paris Olympics, the men's 100 meters freestyle swimming gold was won with the first Olympic time under one minute; who won it?

6) What country has won the most Winter Olympics medals?

7) At which Olympics did Jean-Claude Killy win three skiing gold medals?

8) Who won gold medals in the 5000 meters, 10,000 meters, and marathon races in the 1952 Helsinki games despite never having run a marathon in competition before?

9) At the 1988 Calgary Olympics, officials were so concerned about Mexican cross-country skier Roberto Alvarez during the 50 km race that they did what?

10) What country hosted the first Winter Olympics?

Quiz 6 Answers

1) Bob Mathias (U.S.) - 1948 and 1952

2) Carl Lewis – United States

3) 11 years old – She finished in last place but went on to win gold in subsequent games.

4) Nadia Comaneci – 1976 Montreal

5) Johnny Weissmuller

6) Norway

7) 1968 Grenoble

8) Emil Zatopek – Czechoslovakia

9) They sent out a search party. He had never skied more than 20 km, and officials thought he was lost or injured; he finished more than an hour behind the second to last place finisher.

10) France – Chamonix

Quiz 7

1) What is the only country to have won medals in the Winter Olympics but never in the Summer Olympics?

2) Since the start of the Winter Olympics, how many athletes have won medals at both the winter and summer games?

3) What was the first Asian country to compete in the Olympics?

4) What American has the most Winter Olympics medals?

5) In the 1956 Melbourne Olympics, the equestrian events took place in Stockholm, Sweden; why?

6) What Ethiopian set world records in the men's 5000 meters and 10,000 meters runs in 2008 in Beijing?

7) What year was the Olympic oath first said?

8) What year did the biathlon debut at the Winter Olympics?

9) What U.S. city was first to host the Olympics?

10) Who was the first athlete to win gold medals in five consecutive Olympics?

Quiz 7 Answers

1) Liechtenstein

2) Five – Eddie Eagan (U.S.), Jacob Tullin Thams (Norway), Christa Luding-Rothenburger (East Germany), Clara Hughes (Canada), Lauryn Williams (U.S.)

3) Japan – 1912 Stockholm

4) Apolo Anton Ohno – eight medals from 2002 to 2010 in short track speed skating

5) Australia's quarantine regulations – Australia had a strict six-month quarantine for horses entering the county and would not change it for the Olympics, so Stockholm was selected as the alternate venue for the equestrian events.

6) Kenenisa Bekele

7) 1920

8) 1960 Squaw Valley, California

9) St. Louis – 1904

10) Steven Redgrave (Great Britain) – rowing from 1984 to 2000

Quiz 8

1) Who won the Olympic decathlon gold medal in 1980 and 1984?

2) In addition to his Olympic swimming medals, Johnny Weissmuller won an Olympic medal in what other sport?

3) What are the colors of the five colored rings on the Olympic flag?

4) What is the highest elevation city to host the Summer Olympics?

5) Who is the only male diver to ever sweep the diving events at consecutive games?

6) Famous pediatrician and author Benjamin Spock won an Olympic gold medal in what sport?

7) Who was the first track and field athlete to win at least four gold medals in a single Olympics?

8) How many disciplines are there in men's gymnastics?

9) Among countries that have won at least one Olympic medal, what country has the lowest number of medals per capita?

10) Ski jumping and cross-country skiing are combined into what Olympic sport?

Quiz 8 Answers

1) Daley Thompson – Great Britain

2) Water polo – bronze in 1924

3) Blue, yellow, black, green, red

4) Mexico City – 7,382 feet

5) Greg Louganis – 1984 Los Angeles and 1988 Seoul

6) Rowing

7) Alvin Kraenzlein (U.S.) – four golds in 1900 Paris Olympics

8) Six – vault, rings, floor, high bar, parallel bars, horse

9) India

10) Nordic combined

Quiz 9

1) The famous black power salute of Tommie Smith and John Carlos at the 1968 Mexico City games took place at the medal ceremony for what event?

2) How many throwing events are there in a decathlon?

3) What is the only host country not to win a gold medal at its own Summer Olympics?

4) Where are the headquarters of the International Olympic Committee?

5) Because he was afraid of flying, what did Cassius Clay (Muhammad Ali) wear on his flight to Rome for the 1960 Olympics?

6) At which games was the Olympic flame first used?

7) Who is the only person to win the Olympic marathon twice in a row?

8) What were the first Olympics televised in the U.S.?

9) What is the record for most Olympic medals won in a career?

10) Who has won the most track and field gold medals in a single Olympics?

Quiz 9 Answers

1) Track and field 200 meters - Tommie Smith won the gold; John Carlos won the bronze.

2) Three – discus, shot put, javelin

3) Canada – 1976 Montreal

4) Lausanne, Switzerland

5) Parachute

6) 1928 Amsterdam

7) Abebe Bikila - 1960 Rome and 1964 Tokyo

8) Squaw Valley, California - 1960 Winter Olympics

9) 28 - Michael Phelps in swimming from 2004-2016

10) Paavo Nurmi (Finland) - five golds in 1924 Paris Olympics

Quiz 10

1) When was the last time the Summer and Winter Olympics were held in the same year?

2) What British 400 meters sprinter is remembered fondly for his race at the 1992 Barcelona games where he needed his father's assistance to get to the finishing line after tearing his hamstring?

3) What triple Olympic gold medalist had a daughter who became a

princess?

4) What individual won the most Olympic medals at the 2010 Vancouver Winter Olympics?

5) What year were the first Winter Olympics held?

6) In what Olympics did U.S. sprinter Wilma Rudolph win three gold medals?

7) What two American athletes tied for the second most gold medals in Rio de Janeiro in 2016 with four golds each?

8) What was the first team sport added to the Olympics?

9) What was the first year that professionals could compete in the Olympics?

10) Who is the only person to win four track and field individual (excluding relays and team events) gold medals in a single Olympics?

Quiz 10 Answers

1) 1992

2) Derek Redmond

3) John B. Kelly Sr. – He won golds in the single and double sculls in 1920 Antwerp and gold in the double sculls in 1924 Paris and was the father of actress Grace Kelly who became Princess of Monaco.

4) Marit Bjorgen (Norway) - five medals (three gold, one silver, one bronze) in cross-country skiing

5) 1924

6) 1960 Rome

7) Katie Ledecky (swimming) and Simone Biles (gymnastics)

8) Soccer – 1900

9) 1984 Los Angeles

10) Alvin Kraenzlein (U.S.) – four golds in 60 meters, 110 meters hurdles, 200 meters hurdles, and long jump in 1900 Paris Olympics

Quiz 11

1) What two athletes are tied for the most track and field career gold medals?

2) How many sports were included in the first modern Olympics in 1896?

3) What was the first city to host two Olympics?

4) From 1896 through 2016, how many countries have hosted the Summer Olympics?

5) Which Olympics was the first where every participating country had at least one female athlete on their team?

6) What was the first games where the Olympic torch relay was used to light the flame?

7) In a single Olympics, what is the largest number of different sports a single competitor has won medals in?

8) What sport features a series of bouts known as a barrage?

9) At the famous black power salute medal ceremony at the 1968 Mexico City Olympics, who was the third person on the podium with Tommie Smith and John Carlos?

10) What sport are Torvill and Dean famous for?

Quiz 11 Answers

1) Paavo Nurmi (Finland) - nine golds from 1920-1928 and Carl Lewis (U.S.) - nine golds from 1984-1996

2) Nine - track and field, cycling, fencing, gymnastics, tennis, swimming, shooting, weightlifting, wrestling

3) Paris - 1900, 1924

4) 19 - Greece, France, United States, United Kingdom, Sweden, Belgium, Netherlands, Germany, Finland, Australia, Italy, Japan, Mexico, Canada, USSR, South Korea, Spain, China, Brazil

5) 2012 London - Saudi Arabia, Qatar, and Brunei sent female athletes for the first time.

6) 1936 Berlin

7) Three – American Frank Kugler won medals in freestyle wrestling, weightlifting, and tug of war in the 1904 St. Louis games.

8) Fencing

9) Peter Norman (Australia) - silver medalist

10) Ice dancing

Quiz 12

1) What was the first city to host the Winter Olympics twice?

2) Since tennis returned to the Olympics in 1988, who was the first

American woman to win the singles gold medal?

3) Who was the first woman to win speed skating gold medals at three straight Olympics?

4) What American female track and field athlete has the most career Olympic medals?

5) What country has won the second most Summer Olympics medals?

6) What track and field athlete won gold in both the 200 meters and 400 meters in the 1996 Atlanta Olympics?

7) What water based individual event only appeared in three Olympics from 1984 to 1992 with the United States, Canada, and Japan as the only country who won medals?

8) In what year did softball make its Olympic debut as a medal event?

9) What year was the first Olympic athlete disqualified for drug use?

10) Who was the goalie for the United States hockey team in their gold medal run in the 1980 Lake Placid Olympics?

Quiz 12 Answers

1) St. Moritz, Switzerland – 1928 and 1948

2) Jennifer Capriati – 1992 Barcelona

3) Bonnie Blair (U.S.) – 1988, 1992, 1994

4) Allyson Felix – eight medals (five gold, three silver) from 2004 to 2016

5) Russia

6) Michael Johnson – U.S.

7) Solo synchronized swimming

8) 1996 Atlanta

9) 1968 Mexico City – excessive alcohol

10) Jim Craig

Quiz 13

1) Athens was the site for the first modern Olympics in 1896; what year did the Olympics return to Athens for a second time?

2) What year was the first time Olympic competitors were representatives of countries and not just clubs or individuals?

3) How many players are there on a water polo team?

4) What three cities hosted the Winter Olympics twice in the 20th century?

5) John Akhwari of Tanzania ran the marathon in the 1968 Mexico City Olympics and finished more than an hour behind the winner; yet, he was hailed as an Olympic hero and a symbol of the spirit of the games; why?

6) What is the last event in the decathlon?

7) Who was the first winner of the women's Olympic marathon?

8) What five disciplines make up the modern pentathlon?

9) Who was the third person to win at least six gold medals at a single Olympics?

10) What city hosted the first winter Olympics in Asia?

Quiz 13 Answers

1) 2004

2) 1908 London

3) Seven

4) St. Moritz, Switzerland (1928, 1948), Lake Placid, United States (1932, 1980), Innsbruck, Austria (1964, 1976)

5) After an accident during the race, he ran the last 14 miles with a dislocated knee. When asked later why he kept going, he said, "My country did not send me 9,000 miles to start the race; they sent me 9,000 miles to finish the race."

6) 1500 meters

7) Joan Benoit – 1984 Los Angeles

8) Shooting, swimming, fencing, equestrian show jumping, and running

9) Vitaly Scherbo (Unified Team) - six gymnastics golds in 1992 Barcelona

10) Sapporo, Japan – 1972

Quiz 14

1) What Winter Olympics athlete has the most career medals?

2) Who was the first woman to win nine gold medals over her career?

3) In the first Winter Olympics, what country defended a title that it had won at the prior Summer Olympics?

4) What race was increased by 385 yards, so Edward VII could see the finish line better?

5) Who was the first woman to win at least five gold medals at a single Olympics?

6) What male athlete has the most career winter games medals?

7) In inches, how tall are the hurdles in a men's 110 meters hurdle race?

8) Who was the first woman to win at least four gold medals at a single Olympics?

9) In what year were Jim Thorpe's 1912 gold medals in the decathlon and pentathlon restored to him after he was stripped of them for playing semi-professional baseball prior to the Olympics?

10) What was the first Olympics to include competitors from all six continents?

Quiz 14 Answers

1) Marit Bjorgen (Norway) - 15 cross country skiing medals from 2002-2018

2) Larisa Latynina (Soviet Union) - nine gold medals in gymnastics from 1956-1964

3) Canada - They defended their hockey title; hockey was moved from the summer to the winter games with the first Winter Olympics.

4) Marathon at the 1908 London Olympics - 26 miles 385 yards became the standard distance thereafter.

5) Kristin Otto (East Germany) - six golds in swimming at 1988 Seoul Olympics

6) Ole Einar Bjorndalen (Norway) - 13 biathlon medals from 1998-2014

7) 42 inches

8) Fanny Blankers-Koen (Netherlands) - four golds in track and field at 1948 London Olympics

9) 1982 - They were restored posthumously.

10) 1912 Stockholm

Quiz 15

1) In which winter team sport is pebbling part of the preparation?

2) Who was the first athlete to win the 5000 and 10,000 meter runs in

consecutive Olympics?

3) The 1944 Olympics were canceled due to WWII; in what city were they going to be held?

4) Who was the first American woman to win five career gold medals?

5) Gillis Grafstrom won a gold medal in the same event in both the Summer and Winter Olympics; what event was it?

6) Alistair Brownlee of Great Britain won gold medals in London in 2012 and in Rio de Janeiro in 2016, and his brother Jonathan won bronze and silver in the same games; what sport do the brothers compete in?

7) Which Roman emperor abolished the ancient games in 339?

8) What two German brothers won the Olympic discus gold medals in 2012 and 2016?

9) What team sport was transferred from the Summer Olympics to the Winter Olympics in 1924?

10) What is interesting about the names of the Summer Olympics host cities from 1968 to 1980?

Quiz 15 Answers

1) Curling – Pebbling the ice is done to create some friction for the stone to curl; ice preparers sprinkle the ice with tiny water droplets which freeze on the surface of the ice to create a pebbled texture.

2) Lasse Viren (Finland) – 1972 Munich and 1976 Montreal

3) London

4) Bonnie Blair – speedskating from 1988-1994

5) Figure skating – He won a gold medal in the 1920 Antwerp Summer games before figure skating was moved to the Winter Olympics in 1924 where he won gold again. He also repeated as gold medalist in 1928.

6) Triathlon

7) Theodosius I – He was a Christian and abolished the games because of their pagan influences.

8) Robert Harting (2012) and Christoph Harting (2016)

9) Ice hockey

10) They all start with the letter "M" – Mexico City, Munich, Montreal, Moscow.

Quiz 16

1) Who won three gold medals in half-pipe snowboarding in 2006, 2010, and 2018?

2) Who was the first track and field athlete to win four consecutive gold medals in the same event?

3) Who was the only female athlete at the 1976 Montreal Olympics not given a sex test?

4) What two American athletes tied for the most gold medals at four each at the 2012 London Olympics?

5) Who won the gold medal in men's basketball at the boycotted 1980 Moscow games?

6) At the first modern Olympics, what was awarded to winners?

7) What American track and field athlete has the most career Olympic medals?

8) Who was head of the committee that organized the opening day ceremonies for the 1960 Squaw Valley, California Winter Olympics?

9) In the 1908 London Olympics, a team of eight London policemen beat a team of Liverpool policemen for the gold medal, and a third team of British policemen won the bronze in what sport that was discontinued in 1920?

10) What Olympics were the first to feature active NBA players on the U.S. team?

Quiz 16 Answers

1) Shaun White – U.S.

2) Al Oerter (U.S.) – discus from 1956 to 1968

3) Princess Anne of Great Britain – She competed in equestrian.

4) Michael Phelps and Missy Franklin – both in swimming

5) Yugoslavia - They became only the third country after the U.S. and Soviet Union to win a men's basketball gold medal.

6) Silver medals – Second place received bronze medals.

7) Carl Lewis - 10 medals (nine gold, one silver) from 1984 to 1996

8) Walt Disney

9) Tug of war - There was no limit on the number of teams a nation could enter which resulted in the British sweep of the medals.

10) 1992 Barcelona

Quiz 17

1) Which sprinter won a silver medal in the 1988 Seoul 100 meters and a gold medal in the 1992 Barcelona 100 meters, but was disqualified for two false starts in the 1996 Atlanta 100 meters final?

2) Who first flopped to win the 1968 Olympic high jump gold medal?

3) How much does a U.S. athlete get for winning an Olympic gold medal?

4) What is the only country to win a gold medal at every Summer Olympics?

5) What three countries have won more medals at the Winter Olympics than at the Summer Olympics?

6) What individual won the most Olympic medals at the 2018 PyeongChang Winter Olympics?

7) Who is the oldest Olympic swimmer to win a medal?

8) Who was the only Olympic medalist to also win a Nobel Prize?

9) At the ancient Olympic games, what did they use as archery targets?

10) Who has the second most career Olympic medals?

Quiz 17 Answers

1) Linford Christie – Great Britain

2) Dick Fosbury – He invented the Fosbury Flop which is now the standard for high jumpers.

3) $25,000

4) Great Britain - Due to boycotts, only Great Britain, France, Australia, Greece, and Switzerland have participated in every Summer Olympics.

5) Norway, Austria, Liechtenstein

6) Marit Bjorgen (Norway) - five medals (two gold, one silver, two bronze) in cross-country skiing

7) Dara Torres – 41 years old

8) Philip Noel-Baker (Great Britain) - He won a silver medal in the 1500 meters run in 1920 and the Nobel Peace Prize in 1959.

9) Tethered doves

10) Larisa Latynina (Soviet Union) - 18 medals in gymnastics from

1956–1964

Quiz 18

1) What was the first Olympics where athletes marched into the stadium behind their flags?

2) What sport returned to the Olympics in 1972 after a 52-year absence?

3) Who was disqualified for performance enhancing drugs after winning the men's 100 meters at the 1988 Seoul games?

4) Who won the 400 meters hurdles at the 1976 and 1984 games and had an unprecedented streak of 122 races without a loss?

5) Who was the first athlete to light the Olympic flame and win a gold medal at the same games?

6) What year were the first modern Olympics held?

7) Why did the Russian Olympic team arrive 12 days late for the 1908 London Olympics?

8) American Trischa Zorn earned 55 Paralympic medals over seven games from 1980-2004 in what sport?

9) Who was the first woman to repeat as Olympic champion in the women's heptathlon?

10) Who was the second person to win at least six gold medals at a single Olympics?

Quiz 18 Answers

1) 1908 London

2) Archery

3) Ben Johnson - Canada

4) Edwin Moses – U.S.

5) Cathy Freeman (Australia) – She won the 400 meters race in 2000 in Sydney.

6) 1896 Athens

7) Russia was still using the Julian calendar instead of Gregorian.

8) Swimming

9) Jackie Joyner-Kersee (U.S.) - 1988 Seoul and 1992 Barcelona

10) Kristin Otto (East Germany) – six swimming golds in 1988 Seoul

Quiz 19

1) Barring rain, what is the only track & field event where you get wet?

2) What is the only country to win a gold medal at every Winter Olympics?

3) What happened to the Olympic teams for East Germany and West Germany between 1956 and 1964?

4) What year did China make its first appearance in the Summer Olympics?

5) Frenchwoman Micheline Ostermeyer won the shot put and discus at the 1948 London Olympics; she also had a demanding day job; what was it?

6) Who was the first person to win at least six gold medals at a single Olympics?

7) What are the three weapons used in fencing?

8) What city was scheduled to host the 1940 Olympics canceled due to WWII?

9) What famous philosopher was a double winner at the ancient Olympics?

10) Who won the women's singles gold medal when tennis returned to the Olympics in 1988?

Quiz 19 Answers

1) Steeplechase

2) United States

3) They were joined together into a single German team; political tension tore the teams apart again after 1964.

4) 1984

5) Concert pianist – She had never picked up a discus until a few weeks before winning the Olympic title; she also won bronze in the 80 meters hurdles.

6) Mark Spitz (U.S.) – seven gold medals in swimming at 1972 Munich Olympics

7) Epee, foil, saber

8) Tokyo, Japan

9) Plato – He won in pankration which was a submission sport

combining elements of wrestling and boxing but with very few rules; only eye gouging and biting were banned.

10) Steffi Graf – West Germany

Quiz 20

1) Tennis star Andre Agassi's father competed for Iran in the 1948 and 1952 Olympics in what sport?

2) How many Olympic games have been hosted in Africa?

3) What year were women first allowed to compete in the modern Olympics?

4) Only three people have won individual gold medals in the same event in four consecutive Olympics, who are they?

5) What metal currently makes up 92.5% of an Olympic gold medal?

6) In what event did Baron Pierre de Coubertin, founder of the modern Olympics, win a gold medal at the 1912 games?

7) How many gold medals did Usain Bolt win in the 100 meters, 200 meters, and 4 x 100 meters relay between 2008 and 2016?

8) What was the first U.S. city to host the Olympics twice?

9) What did Abebe Bikila go without in winning the 1960 Olympic marathon?

10) What international incident prompted the 1980 Moscow Olympics boycott?

Quiz 20 Answers

1) Boxing

2) Zero

3) 1900

4) Michael Phelps (swimming 200-meters individual medley), Carl Lewis (long jump), Al Oerter (discus)

5) Silver

6) Mixed literature – Art competition was introduced in 1912 and continued in the Olympics through 1948; Coubertin won for a poem.

7) Eight – He initially won all nine events over the three Olympics, but his first 4 x 100 gold was taken away due to a doping violation by a teammate.

8) Lake Placid – 1932 and 1980

9) Shoes – He ran barefoot.

10) Soviet Union's 1979 invasion of Afghanistan

Quiz 21

1) Who was the first Olympic boxing gold medalist to also win a boxing world championship?

2) What pair won the ice dancing gold medal at the 1984 Sarajevo Olympics?

3) When was the first automatic timing and photo finish system introduced in the Olympics for track events?

4) Over what distance is a human steeplechase run?

5) Who was the first American woman to win three gold medals in a single Olympics?

6) What country has won the most Summer Olympics medals?

7) Who was the first American woman to win the women's gymnastics all-around gold medal?

8) What city was scheduled to host the 1916 Olympics canceled due to WWI?

9) How many cities have hosted the Olympics more than once?

10) Who was the first person to win at least four gold medals at a single Winter Olympics?

Quiz 21 Answers

1) Floyd Patterson – 1952 Olympics and 1956 world champion

2) Jayne Torvill and Christopher Dean - Great Britain

3) 1912 Stockholm

4) 3,000 meters

5) Wilma Rudolph – 1960 Rome Olympics in track and field

6) United States

7) Mary Lou Retton – 1984 Los Angeles

8) Berlin, Germany

9) Seven – Athens, London, Paris, St. Moritz, Lake Placid, Los Angeles, Innsbruck

10) Eric Heiden (U.S.) – five speed skating gold medals in 1980 Lake

Placid Olympics

Quiz 22

1) Mark Spitz was the first and Michael Phelps was the third male swimmer to win at least five gold medals at the same Olympics; who was the second?

2) What is the Olympic motto?

3) What was the first Olympics to feature a 400-meter running track?

4) What was the name of the terrorist group responsible for the violence at the 1972 Munich Olympics?

5) At the 1908 London Olympics, Italian Dorando Pietri was the first marathon runner to cross the finish line but was disqualified for what reason?

6) Who is the first woman to win gold medals in two different sports at the same Winter Olympics?

7) What Australian was the first woman to swim the 100 meters freestyle in under one minute in the Olympics?

8) Who is the first person to win a medal in six straight Summer Olympics?

9) The three-day equestrian event includes show jumping, cross country, and what?

10) Who was the first person to win at least five gold medals at a single Olympics?

Quiz 22 Answers

1) Matt Biondi (U.S.) – five gold medals in 1988 Seoul

2) Faster, higher, stronger or citius, altius, fortius in Latin

3) 1928 Amsterdam

4) Black September

5) He collapsed from exhaustion while finishing in the stadium and was helped up and essentially carried across the line by officials.

6) Ester Ledecka (Czech Republic) - 2018 PyeongChang Olympics in skiing and snowboarding

7) Dawn Fraser - 1964 Tokyo

8) Kim Rhode (U.S.) - skeet shooter from 1996 to 2016

9) Dressage

10) Anton Heida (U.S.) – five gymnastics golds at 1904 St. Louis Olympics

Quiz 23

1) What is the first event in the decathlon?
2) What individual won the most Olympic medals at the 2014 Sochi Winter Olympics?
3) What is the most common surname for an Olympic athlete?
4) What two countries have won three Olympic soccer gold medals?
5) What team sport appeared in the Olympics five times between 1900 and 1936 with Great Britain winning three of the gold medals and Argentina winning the other two?
6) One of the greatest Olympic athletes ever was known as the Flying Finn; who was he?
7) Who was the first African American woman to win an Olympic medal?
8) Who is the only person to win gold medals in both the Winter and Summer Olympics?
9) How many times have the Winter and Summer games been held in the same country in the same year?
10) What is the record for most Olympic gold medals won in a career?

Quiz 23 Answers

1) 100 meters
2) Ireen Wust (Netherlands) – five medals (two gold and three silver) in speed skating
3) Kim
4) Great Britain (1900, 1908, and 1912) and Hungary (1952, 1964, 1968)
5) Polo
6) Paavo Nurmi – Finnish middle and long-distance runner
7) Audrey Patterson – She won a bronze medal in the 200 meters race at the 1948 London Olympics.
8) Eddie Eagan (U.S.) – boxing (1920) and bobsled (1932)
9) Three – 1924 Paris and Chamonix, 1932 Los Angeles and Lake Placid, 1936 Berlin and Garmisch-Partenkirchen

10) 23 – Michael Phelps in swimming from 2004–2016

Quiz 24

1) American Apolo Anton Ohno won eight medals from 2002–2010 in what sport?
2) What Olympic sport allowed professionals for the first time in 2016?
3) In what year did Eddie the Eagle Edwards leap to stardom at the Winter Olympics?
4) In wrestling, how many points is an escape worth?
5) How many perfect 10 scores did gymnast Nadia Comaneci receive at the 1976 Montreal Olympics?
6) What is the only Olympic sport that still bans professionals?
7) What year is the oldest recorded date for the ancient Olympics?
8) What was the first Summer Olympics to be held entirely during the winter?
9) The United States lost the men's basketball gold medal for the first time ever at what Olympics?
10) What city hosted the Winter Olympics only two years after the previous Winter Olympics?

Quiz 24 Answers

1) Short track speed skating
2) Boxing
3) 1988 Calgary
4) One point
5) Seven
6) Wrestling
7) 776 BC
8) 2016 Rio de Janeiro – The other two Summer Olympics in the Southern Hemisphere had taken place at least partly in the spring.
9) 1972 Munich
10) Lillehammer (1994) – It was only two years after the Albertville games because the International Olympic Committee wanted the summer and winter games to be two years apart rather than in the same years.

Quiz 25

1) How many times have the Olympics been canceled?

2) What is the longest track and field race in the Olympics?

3) What American speed skater won five gold medals at the 1980 Lake Placid Olympics?

4) How many times has the United States hosted either the Summer or Winter Olympics?

5) What is the first city to host the Olympics three times?

6) Who was the first American female gymnast to win multiple gold medals in a single Olympics?

7) In the first modern Olympics in Athens in 1896, the most famous host country winner was Spyridon Louis; what event did he win?

8) What gymnastics discipline was contested for the first time at the 1984 Los Angeles games?

9) What husband and wife both won gold medals at the 1952 Helsinki Summer Olympics?

10) Who is the first female to win individual gold medals at four consecutive Olympics?

Quiz 25 Answers

1) Three – 1916, 1940, 1944

2) 50-kilometer walking race

3) Eric Heiden

4) Eight (four summer, four winter) - 1904 St. Louis, 1932 Lake Placid, 1932 Los Angeles, 1960 Squaw Valley, 1980 Lake Placid, 1984 Los Angeles, 1996 Atlanta, 2002 Salt Lake City

5) London – 1908, 1948, 2012

6) Shannon Miller – two golds in 1996 Atlanta

7) Marathon

8) Rhythmic

9) Emil and Dana Zatopek - Emil won the 5,000 meters, 10,000 meters, and marathon despite never running a marathon before; Dana won the javelin.

10) Kaori Icho (Japan) - wrestling from 2004-2016

Quiz 26

1) What movie Tarzan won the 400 meters freestyle swim in the 1932 Olympics?

2) What were the first Olympics held in Asia?

3) What year did badminton debut at the Olympics?

4) What individual won the most gold medals at the 2016 PyeongChang Summer Olympics?

5) In the first modern Olympics in 1896, women were not allowed to compete, but one woman, Stamata Revithi, participated in an unofficial event; what was it?

6) Since tennis returned to the Olympics in 1988, who is the first American man to win the singles gold medal?

7) Since tennis returned to the Olympics in 1988, who is the first man to win the singles title twice?

8) In the 1932 Los Angeles games, the men's steeplechase finalists ran an extra 364 yards; why?

9) What are the seven events in the women's track and field heptathlon?

10) At the 1948 London Olympics, a 30-year-old mother of two earned the nickname "the flying housewife"; who was she?

Quiz 26 Answers

1) Buster Crabbe

2) 1964 Tokyo

3) 1992 Barcelona

4) Michael Phelps (U.S.) – five golds in swimming

5) Marathon – it was run the day after the men's marathon and did not finish in the stadium.

6) Andre Agassi – 1996 Atlanta

7) Andy Murray – Great Britain

8) The race official lost track of the laps, and the entire field ran an extra lap.

9) 100 meters hurdles, high jump, shot put, 200 meters, long jump, javelin, 800 meters

10) Fanny Blankers-Koen (Netherlands) – She won four gold medals in track and field.

Quiz 27

1) Who scored the winning goal for the United States in the "Miracle on Ice" hockey game against the Soviet Union in 1980?

2) How many countries boycotted the 1980 Moscow Olympics?

3) What country was the first to win the women's 10,000 meters race in three consecutive Olympics?

4) What U.S. city has hosted two winter Olympics?

5) Who was the first American cross-country skier to win an Olympic medal?

6) In what year did men's basketball debut as a medal event?

7) Who broke the world record over 30 times in the pole vault and won the gold medal in Seoul in 1988?

8) What 10 events make up the decathlon?

9) What American athlete was originally forced to return his Olympic gold medals after it was learned he had played semi-pro baseball?

10) Where is the Olympic torch originally lit to start its relay to the host site?

Quiz 27 Answers

1) Mike Eruzione

2) 65 - 80 countries sent athletes.

3) Ethiopia - 2008, 2012, 2016

4) Lake Placid – 1932 and 1980

5) Bill Koch - silver medal in 30 km race in 1976 Innsbruck Olympics

6) 1936 Berlin

7) Sergey Bubka – Soviet Union

8) 100 meters, 400 meters, 1500 meters, 110 meters hurdles, long jump, high jump, pole vault, shot put, discus, javelin

9) Jim Thorpe – decathlon and pentathlon gold medalist in 1912 Stockholm

10) Temple of Hera in Olympia, Greece

Quiz 28

1) When Mark Spitz won seven swimming gold medals in a single Olympics, in how many of the events did he break the world

record?

2) What were the first televised Olympics?

3) How many U.S. cities have hosted the Summer Olympics?

4) In the ancient Olympics, women weren't allowed to participate or even be in the stadium, but they could still win the Olympic prize in which event?

5) In what two Olympic sports do men and women compete head to head?

6) From 1900 to 1908, Ray Ewry won eight track and field gold medals in what jumping events that were discontinued in 1912?

7) What Austrian skier won four consecutive men's downhill world titles from 1975-1978, and won gold in the 1976 Innsbruck Olympic downhill?

8) Gold medals were solid gold through what year?

9) Who has won the most gymnastics gold medals at a single Olympics?

10) What was the only Olympics where a single event was held in two different countries?

Quiz 28 Answers

1) Seven

2) 1936 Berlin

3) Three – St. Louis (1904), Los Angeles (1932, 1984), and Atlanta (1996)

4) Chariot racing – The prize went to the owner of the chariot and horse, so women could and did win the prize.

5) Equestrian and sailing

6) Standing long jump, standing high jump, and standing triple jump – They were the same as today's events, but the athlete started in the standing position with no approach run.

7) Franz Klammer

8) 1912

9) Vitaly Scherbo (Unified Team) - six golds in 1992 Barcelona

10) 1920 Antwerp - The 12-foot dinghy sailing event early races were held in Belgium, but the final two races were held in the Netherlands since the only two remaining competitors were Dutch.

Made in the USA
Middletown, DE
12 December 2019